Gathering

Gathering
Family, Grief, Resilience

By Patsy Truxaw

Demitasse Press
SAN LUIS OBISPO

Gathering: Family, Grief, Resilience
ISBN paperback: 979-8-9924284-0-7
ISBN e-book: 979-8-9924284-1-4

All photographs are the property of the author and may not be reproduced without permission. This is a work of nonfiction. The events are portrayed to the best of the author's memory. Dialogue has been reconstructed based on recollection.

For permissions, inquiries, or more information, contact: ptrux@comcast.net

Cover and interior design by Dorka Hegedus
Cyanotype by Annie Neil
Book production by Demitasse Press
Printed in the United States of America, First Edition

Names: Truxaw, Patsy, author.
Title: Gathering : family, grief, resilience / by Patsy Truxaw.
Description: First edition. | Los Osos, CA : Demitasse Press, [2025] | Includes bibliographical references.
Identifiers: ISBN: 979-8-9924284-0-7 (paperback) | 979-8-9924284-1-4 (ebook) | LCCN: 2025902553
Subjects: LCSH: Irish Americans--California--Biography. | Catholics--California--Biography. | Families--California--Biography. | Siblings--Biography. | Resilience (Personality trait) | Bereavement. | Grief. | Addicts--Family relationships. | Mentally ill--Family relationships. | Families of the mentally ill--Biography. | LCGFT: Autobiographies. | BISAC: BIOGRAPHY & AUTOBIOGRAPHY / Memoirs. | FAMILY & RELATIONSHIPS / Death, Grief, Bereavement. | FAMILY & RELATIONSHIPS / Siblings.
Classification: LCC: E184.I6 T78 2025 | DDC: 973/.049162--dc23

For my family, all of you: past, present, and to come

The human heart dares not stay away from that which hurt it most. There is a return journey to anguish that few of us are released from making.

Lillian E. Smith, *Killers of the Dream*

Contents

Cast of Characters

After-school photo in school uniforms taken at Janss Way. Top row, from left: Paul, Bobby, me, Maureen; middle row, from left: Marguerite, Evie, Johnny; bottom row: Michael. Around 1962.

ROBERT JOSEPH (BOB) TRUXAW (MAY 28, 1919–MARCH 13, 1995)

PATRICIA SWEENEY TRUXAW (DECEMBER 21, 1916–AUGUST 1, 2014)

MAUREEN LOUISE TRUXAW (JANUARY 13, 1946–NOVEMBER 7, 2017)

    MARRIED EDWARD SHERLOCK (1971–1985)

        ANNE MAUREEN SHERLOCK (JANUARY 17, 1973)

        ROBERT EDWARD (BOBBY) SHERLOCK (MARCH 21, 1975)

            MARRIED KATIE BOEHM (2008)

                SON JACOB (APRIL 2, 2013)

PATRICIA (PATSY) MARIE TRUXAW (JUNE 6, 1947)

    MARRIED MARK SLAFKES (1976–1980)

    MARRIED JOHN HANSEN (2006)

ROBERT (BOBBY) JOSEPH TRUXAW JR. (SEPTEMBER 18, 1948–SEPTEMBER 19, 1969)

PAUL DENNIS TRUXAW (OCTOBER 8, 1949)

    MARRIED PEGGY HATTON (AUGUST 1972)

        BRIAN WILLIAM (MAY 15, 1978)

        DAVID PAUL (AUGUST 23, 1980)

            PARTNERED SUSIE RICO (2014)

                SON LOGAN (FEBRUARY 26, 2015)

                DAUGHTER EMMA (OCTOBER 30, 2017)

        ERIN MICHELLE (MARCH 17, 1983)

            DAUGHTER CHARLOTTE (APRIL 28, 2025)

EVELYN (EVIE) CAROL TRUXAW (DECEMBER 29, 1951)

    MARRIED MARK PLASSARD (1975–1984)

    MARRIED WAYNE JAMES (2006–2015)

    PARTNERED MARK PLASSARD (2016)

JOHN (JOHNNY) WILLIAM TRUXAW (APRIL 29, 1953)

    MARRIED R. S. (1976–1981)

    MARRIED DAVID WEISS (2008–2020)

MARGUERITE MARY TRUXAW (NOVEMBER 13, 1956)

MICHAEL SWEENEY TRUXAW (NOVEMBER 4, 1960)

Gathering

Introduction

When Mom and Dad brought Michael home from the hospital on November 7, 1960, our family was complete. The next day, we gathered in the family room to watch and celebrate the election of JFK. It seemed like a miracle to our mostly Irish, very Catholic family that this handsome Irish Catholic could be president. A good omen. Michael was an infant and didn't know he was the youngest of eight children; that he would grow up in a crowded, chaotic house—sometimes exhilarating, on occasion scary, and often comforting. I was typically the last person in the house to fall asleep, and the quiet in the house was eerie. Even now, more than sixty years later, I miss the noise, the cacophony of a crowded, hectic house.

We ate dinner at a built-in tan Formica table with benches to accommodate four girls and four boys on opposite sides with parents at the end. There was lots of talk, chatter, and teasing, and always more than one conversation. Sometimes I felt like I needed a helmet. But this was our group, nine or ten of us. A collective brain or consciousness grew from our proximity, fed by our parents' values and road trips in a crowded 1957 Ford station wagon. The music of our noise jostled and bound us for the rest of our lives.

Maureen, the eldest, was bossy and confident. Me, the second child, questioning and observing. Bobby, the first son, good-humored and composed. Paul, the wiggly fourth, often ate at the pullout breadboard. Evie, the fifth in line, cheerful and gabby. Johnny, the sixth, inquisitive and serious. Marguerite, the seventh, white-blonde hair and blue eyes—we called her "the beautiful one." Michael, the eighth, doted upon and talkative.

For almost nine years, our family was whole, if not always in the same place at the same time. And then, in 1969, Bobby died in a car accident the day after his twenty-first birthday. The current between us cracked, leaving static, confusion, and grief as nine lives responded, somewhat together but mostly alone. The sudden loss of a brother and son was pivotal to much of what followed. Some of it was good, and plenty of it was bewildering.

Gathering is my attempt to make sense of and pay homage to the group and its parts. Before I began this project, I thought it was shared loss and grief that kept us together and, over the years, healed any rift or rupture, at least eventually. But now I think our bond is more than one of heartache and sorrow. Maybe it began to form back in that crowded '57 Ford wagon, when we'd each raise ten fingers to the curious looky-loos who gaped at us from other cars. It both amused and annoyed us kids, the stares we got from riders along the road. *How many are in that station wagon anyway?* we imagined them wondering. Our raised fingers were the answer, a gesture of unity and pride. We had a strong sense of the first-person plural. Our "we" was strong.

Our family is affected—or should I say infected—with genetic predispositions to some chemical imbalances in our brains. We have mental illness, addiction, anxiety, depression. "Bad wiring" is how I think of it. You need to know this part of the story. You also need to know we have connection, joy, celebration, success, tragedy, and resilience. We have community, a sense of justice and fairness, social awareness, and conscience. We have activists, educators, lawyers, medical professionals, sales reps, writers, and dreamers. We have Giants, Dodgers, and Padres fans. We are and have pluses and minuses, contradictions.

Gathering isn't a complete family history. It's meant to be slices of life, vignettes that present a mosaic of lives, none of which turned out as expected. All the stories in this book are told from my memory and point of view. I hope they will be entertaining and instructive for present and current generations. One thing I've learned and try to practice is to tell the truth, even when it hurts.

~~~~~~

Chapters of Gathering *were written as separate stories between 2012–2024, with just a few updates until publication.*

Where I'm From

I'm from station wagons and holy cards

Tuna casserole and Velveeta,

From the long beige table

Crowded, Formica, clamor of many voices

I'm from the flowering pear out the kitchen window

Background for Holy Communions,

Graduations, gold cords, handstands, summer shorts, knobby knees, fireworks

I'm from baseball on the transistor radio, World Series on TV, the ten-cent pool

Fall drives during heat waves

All ten of us

A night swim with my father

From Nanas Sweeney and Truxaw, Bob and Pat, a.k.a. Tri

I'm from Grampa-Dad and Patrick, bad wiring, good politics

From always think of others, do your homework and practice,

Comb your hair, don't have weird friends

An excess of Catholic judgment, abundance of love and mixed messages

Denial and good intentions

I'm from Anaheim, the beach house, from Derry and Dublin and Bohemia

Mashed potatoes and backyard peaches, Shrove Tuesday, and strudel

Pianos and cousins and brothers and sisters and diapers and

Don't turn out like Auntie Edna, from

Trains and boats and roadsters, the journey of Patrick and Mary Angela

My mom's laugh

Daddy's bum leg, good eye, and camera

Boxes from the garage, transformed pixels, JPEGs

Images and sounds, memory, and digital recovery

Archives of family history

Roots

March 26, 2018

September 1969

"Let's get out of here," I say to Evie and Johnny.

Our typically chaotic house has been besieged for two days, teeming with aunts, uncles, nanas, cousins, our nuclear family, neighbors, friends. Even Sister Mary David, a beloved teacher from St. Boniface School, stopped by for a visit. Tears, whispers, soothing voices, an occasional cry or wail. Somewhere Uncle Noel is telling Maureen, "You must be strong. Be brave for your mother." An obligation turned resentment my older sister held for the rest of her life. Liquor bottles and snacks litter the kitchen counter, along with ashtrays for Aunt Ailish and Uncle Noel, two of Mom's younger siblings.

The three of us leave, flee.

It's September 1969, a warm late afternoon, and I drive toward the beach—to Corona Del Mar, not Newport, which would be too familiar and sad. We plop down on the sand at a small rocky cove, exhaling shaky sighs. Our backs to the world, eyes fixed toward the open horizon of the ocean. Quiet. Finally, some quiet. Late afternoon waves crawl in and out, growing larger with the tide, reassuring, soothing. We're adjusting to a sudden and irreversible change in our individual and collective lives. The cool damp of the ocean at the end of a warm day, hiss and spray, rushing and shushing. Our hearts are breaking, and we have no language.

In the picture held in my memory, we appear as children, but in fact I was twenty-two; Evie, seventeen; and Johnny, sixteen. We were uniformly thin, narrow, and wiry like Daddy; two blond, one dark Irish like Mom. Our brother Bobby had been slightly heftier and one of six blonds. Even though I was a year older, Bobby had always felt like a big brother. Never temperamental or insecure like I was, he'd had a great ease and kindness about him. He'd been twenty-one for only one day.

We came to the beach rather than go to the funeral parlor. I didn't want to see Bobby's dead, frozen face and had declined what seemed like countless opportunities to do so. I didn't want that image forever lodged in my head. Fifty years later, I've had plenty of time to wonder whether I made the right choice. And even though I loved it, I really needed to get out of that house. I hadn't lived in it for three years by that point. I'd been asleep on a floor in San Francisco when the call came from Daddy at two thirty in the morning the prior Saturday. My friend Amy, wearing a nightgown, drifted out of her room to wake and tell me I had a phone call. Daddy said there'd been an accident, that Bobby had been hurt, that "he didn't make it."

"But I just saw him two days ago," I said.

"We couldn't find you anywhere, Patsy." His voice cracked and broke. "Your brother is dead, and we had to track down Amanda to find where you were. Do you think you'll come home?"

I'd flown to San Francisco to cover a Regents Meeting for the *New University*, the University of California Irvine (UC Irvine) campus newspaper where I was managing editor. I promised I'd be right there, and with Amy's help, I made it onto an Air Cal flight later that morning. Paul, thirteen months younger than Bobby, picked me up at Orange County Airport. Usually such a goof-off, the family clown, he was solemn and quiet. He and Bobby were tight. Paul could be silly because Bobby was so solid. Paul said things were crazy at the house, that it was just really strange, that Mom and Dad were falling apart.

We sit and stare into the Pacific, look at one another, shake heads, sigh, and stare some more. Shorts dampening in the sand; butts falling asleep. How could this have happened?

We know the ocean. We grew up spending the best times of every summer at the family beach house on the Newport boardwalk, which had been in Daddy's family since he was a young man. It was a rambling clapboard bungalow at Thirty-Second Street and the oceanfront until 1963, when it was razed and rebuilt as two modern units. Newport was at most a thirty-minute drive from our home on Janss Way in Anaheim. An old black-and-white family photo shows four carefree children (the first four, Maureen, Patsy, Bobby, Paul) wearing identical swim trunks, arms outstretched, running into the water. Other photos show Mom and aunties looking glamorous for the camera, many small children tumbling over them as they sit on the sand. As teenagers, we sat or lay on the sand clustered with cousins and friends, the group always taking up a large swath of beach. Some of us, including me, lived at the Newport Beach house while in college.

I get up and walk to the water's edge, the water a welcome relief. But I'm too restless to stay there for long. I feel like I'm onstage, acting, like I should know how to behave and feel when I'm so totally lost. When the call had come from Daddy, I'd watched as I flew up and away from myself, disconnected, detached, observing, unsure what my lines should be.

Johnny and Evie still sit on the sand, and I feel the need to say something useful. I am, after all, the eldest one here. I'd seen Bobby two days before the accident. He'd come by my apartment in Newport so I could give him his birthday present: Judy Collins's *Wildflowers*, an album I loved and hoped he'd appreciate. He did like it and said Sue would too. He said other things I wish I could remember. It was a happy, easy conversation, and it felt like a special moment, my brother visiting my place voluntarily.

"What do you think Bobby would want us to be doing?" Evie asks. "He wouldn't want everyone to be all crazy and sad, would he?"

She looks to Johnny and me for agreement. My heart and throat clench. Johnny draws in his breath.

"It's so unbelievable," he says. "He didn't have to go to the football game with Pelle. It was a last-minute thing."

Johnny had been at home on Friday night when the call from the hospital came, along with Marguerite and Michael, the youngest of the eight of us. Maureen, who was no longer living at home, happened to be there too. Johnny recalls that she was the one who answered the phone. Johnny drove Mom and Daddy to a small hospital where Los Angeles meets Orange County. He waited while they waited, helpless to do anything but pray. When Mom and Daddy went with the doctors to see Bobby, Johnny was left alone.

John Pelle was one of Bobby's high school friends and a sportswriter for the local paper. They'd been on their way to an out-of-town school football game, when the passenger side of Pelle's sports car was hit head-on. He'd sat on the curb waiting for help while Bobby was stuck inside the small car with a smashed chest. Pelle, too, was at the hospital and wound up driving my parents and Johnny back to Anaheim later that night. Johnny said he couldn't do it.

I only learned these grim details in recent years. Hearing them stimulated a rekindling of sadness and frustration. That sixteen-year-old Johnny would've been expected to drive our parents and Pelle home after his older brother's sudden death. That the guy who'd been behind the wheel during the fatal accident did drive them home. Why hadn't I known these details earlier? Had I not been paying attention? A recurrence of what-ifs washed over me: What if help had arrived sooner? What if they'd had cell phones? What if the accident had occurred a few years later when EMTs would've been better equipped to save Bobby? If only we hadn't missed out on his whole fucking life. To my knowledge, the family had little further connection with John Pelle. I don't even know if he was at the funeral. It's not that he was blamed for the accident, but what? Was he blamed for surviving?

"I still don't believe it," Evie says. "I just don't believe it. He was here Friday. He was there when I left to go to work the night before last."

"Did he see it coming?" I wonder aloud. He'd been so relaxed and happy. He'd had Sue and UCLA.

"I don't know," Johnny says. "But I think it happened really fast. He would say to take care of Mom, that's for sure. And what about Paul?" he continues in a rush. "He and Bobby are so close. How's he going to get over this?" Johnny takes a breath.

"And Sue, imagine how unbelievable this is for her. To lose her boyfriend. I mean they were practically engaged," Evie says. "And Nana Truxaw, this is going to kill her. She gave him Grampa-Dad's medical bag for his birthday."

"Nobody at the house knows what to do," Johnny says, his voice rising. "Except drink, of course. And eat, cry. Mom keeps saying she can't believe God would do this to someone like Bobby. I think Daddy gave her a Valium."

We yield to the comforting sounds of the nearby ocean, sitting quietly with shattered hearts and disjointed thoughts. Years later, Johnny wouldn't recall having been at the beach, but he would recollect having lain on his stomach on the front lawn, his back to the sky, feeling alone and getting his first glimpse of hell, of inchoate grief and misery.

The three of us sit together until darkness takes most of the light from the sky. Even though I'm unsure what I'm feeling, a touchstone is lodged. In the best way we can manage in this moment, we're recognizing Bobby. That I will never see or hear from him again is unthinkable. We make our way back to the car and home to Anaheim. The funeral is tomorrow.

I'd later learn that Michael, eight years old at the time, was seen walking down the long hall along the bedrooms at Janss Way, alone and crying. I have no recollection of Michael or Marguerite that weekend, and only a vague memory of Maureen. I have an image of all nine of us sitting in the front pew of the church, and I recall the woefully sad organ music.

People streamed by our place of honor in the front row of St. Boniface Church offering their respects at the closed coffin. It was surreal. We listened as Father Quatannens eulogized someone we didn't recognize, his words so generic that Evie and I began whispering in dismay how much Bobby would hate this—and then giggling. If his funeral were held these days, a family member would share escapades and events from his life: Three cousins, Tim, Pat, and Bobby, getting sent home early from school for mischievous behavior; how Bobby and Paul had been so close; the time Bobby was my date to the senior prom. But we were young and uninitiated in death and memorials. Father Quatannens didn't know Bobby. He was the same priest who'd told Daddy he'd be in a state of sin if Daddy sold birth control pills at his drugstore in Garden Grove. We did not like Father Quatannens.

My friend Florence was waiting at the church exit and gave me a long hug as we walked toward our limousine to Holy Sepulcher Cemetery. I loved her for that, even long after she became a Jehovah's Witness and decided we weren't friends anymore. Daddy jumped into the passenger seat of the hearse to ride with Bobby, his junior and first boy; our dad always played a good shepherd. The rest of us followed in the limo.

A smell of burnt leaves mingled with incense at the cemetery in the dry hills above Anaheim. The pastor we loathed swung one of the tools of his trade over the open grave. We stood there numbly as Bobby was lowered into the ground. It had been summer on Bobby's birthday; on the day of the funeral, it was fall.

A few days into the new season, I'd get into my green Volkswagen and head back to the start of my last year at Irvine. Soon, I'd hear "He Ain't Heavy, He's My Brother" by the Hollies on the car radio. The first few times I pulled over to listen and cry. Even though I've often wondered whether it's cheesy, it's still my private song to my brother. It helped me understand what I was feeling back then. Bobby was not too heavy to carry in my heart. I didn't want to let him go and didn't have to, not entirely. I was beginning to learn something about grief.

Everything that came next for us was largely seeded that weekend. It was a moment in time that shaped the definition of who we as family would become.

Newport

The old clapboard-type beach house at 3110 West Oceanfront had a sandy, sticky floor, no matter how frequently it was swept. The traffic of feet from the beach, just steps away, was unrelenting. Even now, more than fifty years later, I could draw the floorplan of this place and describe its furnishings in detail. There was the porch, of course. In fact, two porches, one that started up the steps from the sidewalk, with its half or "pony" wall, over the side of which countless photos show children and adult legs dangling as family members sit and stare out at the water, into the sun. A few of the photos show renegade youth (including my brother Paul) standing barefoot on that half wall. At the back of the porch, there was rattan and wicker furniture, old cushions. It was inviting, slightly sandy—always the sand.

The adjacent sleeping porch was just large enough for a big bed and a small table. We played cards there, listening to the waves just beyond the sidewalk and the beach. We took turns sleeping there too. Once I shared the bed with my cousin Peggy, and I remember waking up and seeing that she was sleeping upside down in the bed, her feet at my head.

Lots of cousins and aunts and uncles at the old beach house. If you look closely, you can see me in the middle leaning against the brick fence in the plaid shorts, with Evie and Maureen on top of and behind the fence. Is that Paul leaning out from the crossbeam? Early 1960s.

Me enjoying the view from the beach house porch. Mid-1950s.

The house itself had three bedrooms, a living room, one bath, a large kitchen. The heart of this house—"dining room" would be too fine a term for it. No, it was an eating and gathering room. Two wall-long benches forming an L bent around dining tables; a few chairs filled the seating gaps, all of it painted blue or green enamel. The space could accommodate a large crowd for meals, maybe twenty at a time if some of the group were children, which in those days some always were. The benches may have been on three sides. I remember my sister Marguerite running around the table once, half-crazed in delight, about three years old, the benches like her runway. She was a gorgeous child.

By the 1960s, the family had gotten too large, the house decrepit in its loveliness. Daddy and his seven siblings decided to tear it down and build a replacement with two units, three bedrooms down, four bedrooms up, the stairway adjoining them sandy. What radiant views we had. Each family spent a week (or more) during the summer, and once we kids were college age, we could rent either the upper or lower during the school year. I was fortunate to live there off and on, and so was Paul. The family sold it in the 1970s. What a bummer.

Today, on a bright late morning or early afternoon when we have a certain kind of heat, if I sit for a minute with my face toward a radiant sun, I'm transported back to a younger self, reclining on a beach towel in front of 3110, a sandy book at hand, toes curling in hot sand, heat on my back, cocooned in a fuzzy-headed warmth of splendid bliss. Newport.

Heat Beat

It was hot. Too hot to work. Too hot to play. Too hot to do anything but think of the heat.

Mom had a solution. We would fix hotdogs and bring them to the beach house for dinner.

It was getting late. Maureen insisted. She did not mind the hot, crowded ride. She wanted to see the cool ocean.

Marguerite and Michael were already fed. Maureen still insisted. Mom, Dad, Maureen, Evie, Johnny, Marguerite, and Michael got into the car. I put on my lipstick and went out also, without my bathing suit. It was too hot to go into the back bathroom and rummage through all the other suits for mine. Anyway, it was too hot to go swimming.

Bobby gave up his homework and got into the car. Paul still held out. I decided to get my bathing suit after all.

We fought over seats. Mom said that Paul could not stay home alone. He said that he could. Mom told him to get into the car. Paul got into the hot, crowded car. We again fought over seats.

We took the hot, crowded ride to the beach. The heat caused us to be cross. We fought. Dad threated to turn around.

Finally, we arrived. We were not the only people trying to escape the heat. Two sets of aunts and uncles and cousins were also at the beach.

Everyone was in the water. I decided that it was not too hot to go swimming.

It was dark. Evie and I, walking into the water, held hands until we saw the others. The cool ocean sent a chilling sensation through us. It was cold.

~~~~~~

Written at age sixteen for Sister Mary Sebastian's journalism class, Marywood High School, Anaheim, California, September 1963.

Bobby

Early one evening in 1968 when I was a student at UC Irvine and renting the upstairs of the family beach house on the oceanfront in Newport, Bobby showed up at the front door. I hadn't been expecting him. *What the hell is he doing here?* I wondered, cautiously opening the door. There he stood on a slightly damp and sandy porch, in a tailored windbreaker of indeterminate color, the sun dropping into the ocean behind him. He looked fresh and clean-cut compared to the longhaired, flannel-shirted, bearded guys sitting on the couch facing the open door. They were smoking cigarettes and drinking red wine; one was sucking on his mustache, and another was holding forth. (We'd been doing a reading of a Lenore Kandel poem.) As Bobby leaned across me to peer inside, one of them said, "Hey, man."

"What happened?" I asked, afraid someone had died or, worse yet, that Mom had sent him to spy on me. I stepped outside and closed the door.

"Are those your friends?" he gasped in unconcealed amazement.

"They're friends from the newspaper," I explained, steering him downstairs and toward the beach.

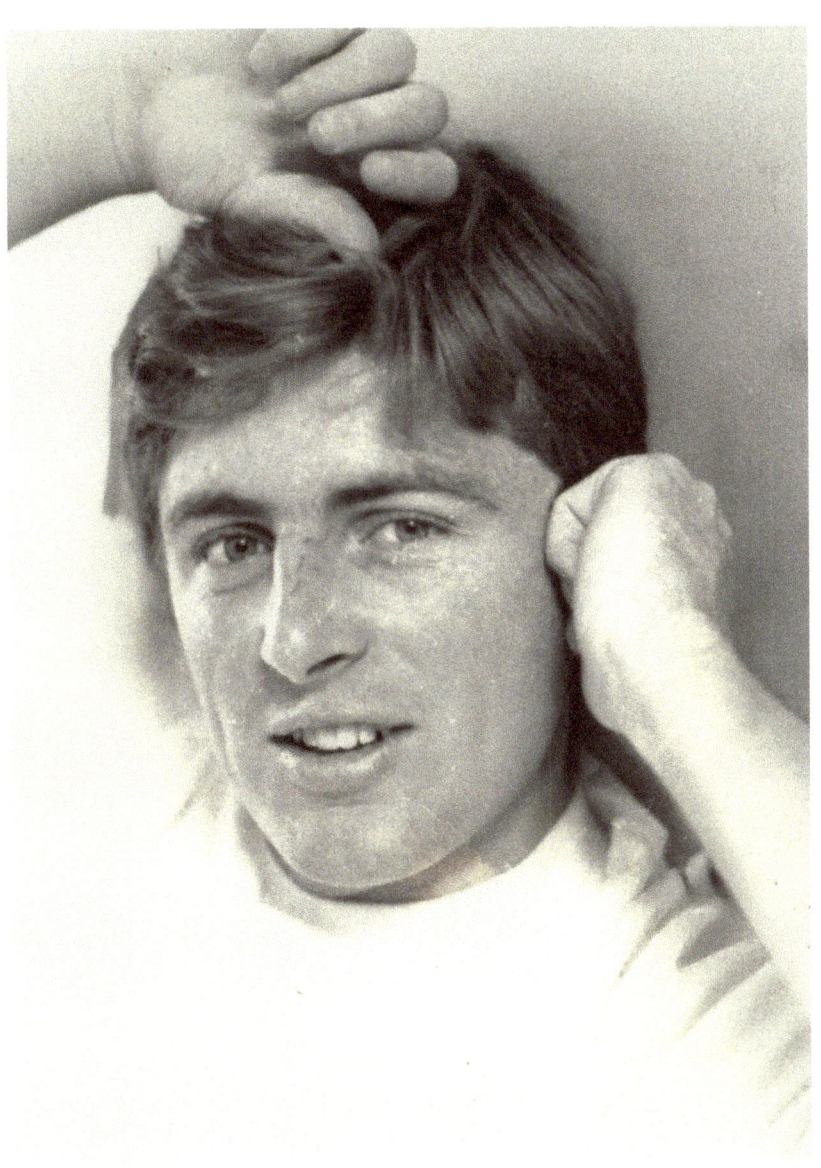

Bobby. Undated.

"We need to talk," he said.

My heart pumped in frustration and suspicion. *Here it comes*, I thought.

"About what you're doing to Mom and to the whole family."

"You don't know what you're talking about," I said. "She's too narrow-minded, and besides, I'm not doing anything bad. They're guys from the school paper."

"You're breaking her heart," he said. "Mom's upset and worried. Don't you care about her? About the rest of us?"

We danced around each other liked wounded birds, spinning in the sand.

"How can you even hang out with them? Those hippies will bring down the property value. You shouldn't be having people like them at the beach house."

"How can you do this?" I yelled. "You're not an idiot, are you? They're not hippies. They're students, just like me."

"But Mom is upset and worried about you."

"Why don't you open your eyes," I pleaded. "Please. The country is falling apart, and this is what matters to you? You're doing Mom's dirty work." I was angry and frustrated. He was my younger brother by a mere fifteen months.

"Try thinking for yourself for once," I sputtered.

"Amanda is a bad influence on you," he retorted.

Amanda, the friend Mom blamed for my fall from the family norm, the friend I went to see the Doors and Jefferson Airplane with. Amanda and I had helped Phil Pearlman, the longhaired editor of UCI's first student newspaper the *Anthill*, and a musician, do light shows in the gym for Janis Joplin and Big Brother and the Holding Company. It was the back half of the sixties. At the time of Bobby's visit, I was fine arts editor of the *New University*, the succeeding student paper. Amanda was managing editor.

He reiterated Mom's litany of my wrongs, including the presumed sex and drugs, warning that I'd be evicted if I didn't clean up my act. No matter how many times I told him he didn't know what he was talking about, he didn't get it. Not yet. He was confused by what was new, what didn't fit in the world of the family and the home on Janss Way.

"Amanda isn't even here," I sighed, exasperated. I don't recall where Amanda was living then, and this isn't about her anyway. It's about Bobby and me, and of course Mom, who was grievously troubled at my rocking the boat. In a year or so Bobby would be out of the house and off to UCLA, where his own eyes and heart would expand.

In retrospect, we were both such innocents then. At the time, though, I was disappointed and felt betrayed. I valued what he thought and what he thought of me. He was the same brother who'd reassured me before my first day at Irvine, after a dermatology treatment had burned off a layer of my acne-stained face, that the freakish peeling didn't show through my makeup. He'd said I looked pretty. He'd also agreeably escorted me and a friend to the joint senior prom for Marywood (girls) and Servite (boys) High Schools. Mom rented him a tux and bought me a long slim dress with embroidered flowers trailing down the side. Besides the dress, the best part about that dance was how good-natured Bobby was.

He was the first brother I'd had rapport with; we were close in age and birth order. We'd played together when we were little, and once he helped me give our two-year old sister Evie a haircut when a game of doctor's office turned into barbershop. We were upstairs at The Old Place, Daddy's grand birth home on what was then Los Angeles Street in Anaheim. We were living there while our future home on Janss Way was being built. Evie played our willing client even as her soft brown curls fell onto the hardwood floor. Mom was horrified when we escorted Evie down the stairs and excitedly introduced her: "Here's your new boy." I was blamed. I must have been six and Bobby five years old. Mom threatened to cancel our week at the beach. I knew she'd tell the aunts and cousins how bad I'd been, so I hid in the lifeguard stand once we got to Newport and everyone began arriving. Blameless Bobby was free to have fun.

Our Janss Way house was in the middle of a short cul-de-sac where boys and girls of all ages, neighbors and cousins, brothers and sisters, congregated to play baseball. Even I participated. The boys played football in our backyard or at the nearby Anaheim High School. As we got older, the guys stuck more to themselves. Early on, Bobby was best friends with our cousins Tim LeVecke and Pat Sweeney. This threesome went through grammar school together, and Tim and Bobby remained close after Pat's family moved away. As I mentioned earlier, Bobby and our brother Paul were a year apart and good buddies, too, though completely different in temperament. Bobby was calm and steady and ready with an occasional smirk; Paul was hyper and goofy.

Disneyland opened in 1955, around the time we moved into Janss Way, and became a fixture in the background of everyone's life in Anaheim. It settled in on the south side of town, not too far from The Old Place, and many acres of orange tree orchards had been sacrificed to build it. To get there from Janss Way was a straight shot down Harbor Boulevard, past Pearson Park, past St. Boniface, beyond Marywood before it moved out of town, across South Street and Ball Road, and over the freeway. While it was eventually embedded between the Santa Ana Freeway and acres of motels, in the early days it loomed, a vast parking lot with the rides and the kingdom visible in the short distance. The Matterhorn and Sky Ride, once built, were notable alterations to Anaheim's otherwise flat skyline.

The thought of entering the Magic Kingdom's gates quickened the heartbeat. Everyone wanted to work at the Magic Kingdom when they were old enough. Maureen got a job in a candy shop on Main Street and wore an early twentieth century shopgirl's frilly white blouse and long candy-striped skirt. I was rejected as a Disneyland employee because I had pierced ears, another indicator that I was an outlier, although we didn't use that word then. No surprise that I wasn't in the mainstream of youth chosen to work at one of the largest employers of teenagers in Anaheim. Bobby readily got hired as a sweeper.

I often drove down Harbor to collect Maureen or Bobby from work, Bobby more often because he was younger and didn't have a car. I remember picking him up one summertime in my first car, a yellow Ford Fairlane that Uncle Jerry had found for me. I'd pull into the flat, blacktop employee lot and watch the exodus of frontiersmen, spacemen, shopgirls, cartoon characters, and others until my brother emerged through the gate wearing his plain custodial uniform. He was lanky and blond, no longer a pudgy kid. He'd gotten handsome. Usually smiling, he'd lumber into the car, thank me for getting him, and tell me about some of the things he'd picked up that day: a man's watch, an earring, gum wrappers, random trash. He didn't seem to mind the menial nature of a job that permitted him to walk around Disneyland for hours sweeping debris into a hinged dustpan while observing a world of tourists and events and fantasy. I was envious.

On our drive back to Janss Way, we would hear the percussion of Disneyland's fireworks begin to rumble. Brilliant lights would erupt and drape down through the night sky, visible in the car's rearview mirror and through the back windows. Such explosions were a nightly occurrence, starting at nine o'clock sharp from Memorial Day through Labor Day. When we were younger, and even later when we were home for it, we would sit on damp grass beneath the flowering pear tree and watch the huge fireworks display. Green, red, gold, blue, and white lights would billow and rise, float and drift, melting down over the just-darkening summer sky—and we on the grass, still wearing shorts, feet bare. The boom of Disney's fireworks would conclude the outside part of our day like a punctuation mark.

It's one of the most satisfying recollections of my childhood, watching night fall from beneath that tree; then getting up, wiping the damp, loose grass from the bottom of my shorts, my legs crinkled and lined with lawn marks, and going inside with my brothers and sisters. That memory is second only to the night drives with my brother. We'd listen to the radio, baseball with Vin Scully and Jerry Doggett if it was on, or maybe KFWB. Or we'd engage in quiet conversation, about the Dodgers, or who was at home, or the events of the day, always with the springing fountains of multicolored light in the background, illuminating the car and us as we made our course, windows open, back to Janss Way.

~~~~~~~~

Attending UC Irvine from 1965 onward was mind-expanding for a Catholic girl, especially at first. I began "educating" siblings and our parents about the evils of the Vietnam War, racism, and more. I gave Bobby *The Prophet* by Kahlil Kibran as a gift for his high school graduation. I lived on Janss Way at first but eventually moved out to be closer to school, friends, and my job on the student newspaper.

In my recollection, it didn't take long for Bobby to evolve away from the young man who knocked on my door to deliver Mom's message about my fall from family grace. During spring break that same year, my parents flew Bobby and me to Portland, where our older sister Maureen was in college—another attempt to get me away from my friends. From Portland, Bobby and I took the train to Seattle to visit the University of Washington, one of the many colleges Daddy had attended while pursuing his postwar pharmacy degree. I have a picture of Bobby gripping his trench coat tightly against the rain as he looks straight into the camera. I had the new Simon & Garfunkel album *Parsley, Sage, Rosemary and Thyme*. In my memory, "Homeward Bound" and "The Dangling Conversation" play in the background on our return train to Portland. The train didn't actually have a stereo system, but that's the soundtrack to my memory. By the end of that trip, Bobby had heard plenty of my side of the story.

He started his own higher education at the local community college, Fullerton Junior College, and then transferred to UCLA to do premed. He didn't grow his hair out or dramatically change his wardrobe or appearance, but Bobby's mind and view of the world expanded when he was out on his own. He started dating. We began hearing about someone named Sue whom he'd met at Weyburn

Hall, the dorm where they both lived. We corresponded those days via mail (how quaint, it seems now), and I heard about her in letters. We planned a time to meet in Westwood, probably at Hamburger Hamlet, and Sue and I were introduced. There was no question of approving of his girl—the way they kept looking at one another and smiling! Sue was a freckled brunette with long hair and a genuine smile, bright, curious, easygoing. My brother had a girlfriend, and it felt right.

I received a birthday card from Bobby for my twenty-second birthday in June 1969, a children's card, a choo-choo train in connecting pieces. It included a chatty letter. He said *The Prophet* had come in handy! He described a party he and Sue attended as something out of Hemingway where everyone was drunk. He'd liked the issues of the *New University* I'd included with a recent letter. He emphasized that he wanted to tell me some things when he saw me. I've managed to save the letter for fifty-five years. It's at the end of this chapter if you want to read it.

Sue was at the beach house with Bobby and some of the family during our annual allotted time in the summer of 1969. She was his date to our cousin Tim LeVecke's wedding that July. And he'd also been to Bakersfield to meet and spend time with her family. Far as I know, they were planning to return to the dorm when school reopened in September. But that was not to be. I saw him the day before his twenty-first birthday, on September 18, when he came to the Newport apartment I shared with Amanda so I could give him that early birthday gift. We had an easy conversation. He already liked the album and said Sue liked it too. He told me he didn't think he wanted to do premed anymore, that he was more interested in the humanities. It was obvious that he'd had a supremely happy summer, and that Sue had become part of his life, and ours. That was the last time I saw him.

June 3, 1969

Dear Patsy,

I hope you have a happy birthday, and here's something to keep you entertained for a while.

I got your papers & your letter today. I was impressed by the paper & I showed it around & people liked it.

So the book you gave me for my graduation, The Prophet, well it's come in handy. I still haven't finished reading it & doubt if I ever will, but the section on Joy & Sorrow came in handy.

If you think I'm going to tell you how it came in handy, you're nuts, but thanks for giving it to me.

Last weekend was a blast. We hit 2 movies (now 3), and we went to a party on Saturday. The party was unbelievable. It was almost out of Hemingway, like the lost generation.

Everybody there (except for one who drove home) was drunk. Someday I'll tell you about it. On Friday I finally saw Dr. Zhivago, and on Sunday we went to Funny Girl, which was good but not as good as Oliver (in my opinion).

I got a letter today from home & Mom said that Daddy had a good time on Wed. What gives? I'd write more but now I'm going to a studio preview & so I've got to go. You may not believe this but I'm not behind in any of my studies. Sue says high, so high.

Later on, I'd like to talk to you about the paper. Maybe I'll write again before I see you, but at the rate I write, I doubt it. So have a happy b.day. I'll be seeing you soon,

Love Bobby

P.S. Thanks for the large envelope. It'll come in handy. Also in 1 month & 2 days Tim L. has had it.

~~~~~~~~~

Tim L is our cousin and the first one in the extended family to get married—one month and a few days after Bobby wrote this letter.

Bobby and Sue at Cousin Tim LeVecke's wedding. July 1969.

Janss Way

Sound was the prevailing sensory feature of life at 549 Janss Way. It was a noisy, hectic house, populated by ten of us at various stages of development, all with our own dissonances and dispositions. Was it happy noise? Sometimes. Mostly. Familiar. On occasion I could've used a bullhorn or a microphone or earplugs.

Who am I if everyone talks at the same time? Who is heard if everyone talks at the same time? The loudest or the wisest? Anyone? I must always chime in, if only to prove I'm there. Words come easily to me. I intrude, change the subject, contradict, question. Yes, I still butt in to conversations, and I apologize for the too many times I've interrupted. It's a learned behavior, a habit, deeply ingrained. Our youngest, Michael, shrieked an indelible and unintelligible sound, harsh and shrill to all ears. "Bwaa, waaah waaah." Sudden quiet. His screech was an admonition to, "Please, won't you all shut up and look at me?" Like the crescendo cries from the pack of coyotes we hear nightly where I live now. It was like this at breakfast and dinner. There's evidence.

Bobby on the phone with (from left) Paul, Marguerite, and Evie. September 18, 1969.

At some point in the early 1960s, Daddy bought a tape recorder, and Johnny later converted one of the recordings to an MP3 he aptly named "Family Chatter." That track, which is a collection of sounds from our home and family life, resides as an anomaly in my Apple Music collection. The "song" is eighty-five minutes long and not so much revelatory as confirmatory of the many layers of sound and cacophony we generated and dwelled in together. It opens on a school day morning in the kitchen. The lower register of boy voices blurs, and with so many of us talking at once, it's difficult to differentiate and discern individual speakers other than those of our parents. Daddy is leaving for work. Mom's pleasant voice surfaces above the clamor as she serves food and makes lunches. A conversation ensues about a new position at the boys' school. Several voices offer opinions, one of them probably mine. Why does Servite need a Dean of Discipline? Michael's piercing three-year-old bleat commands attention.

It's an audio patchwork, haphazard, nonlinear sound bites of family life captured willy-nilly, in the main of children, an exquisite microcosm of our discordant but typically tolerant household.

Judging from some bits of poorly recorded music, and AM radio outtakes splattered throughout ("Days of Wine and Roses," "Our Winter Love"), the year was 1963. There's Maureen playing bursts of classical piano pieces, displaying the talent that garnered her a music scholarship to the University of Portland. Marguerite is goaded by a brother into singing. There's me practicing French (*Où est la bibliothèque?*). Paul and Cousin Jim do silly man-on-the-street interviews, asking people if they prefer the Beach Boys or the Beatles.

I've listened closely in hopes of hearing Bobby's voice, but I can't sort him out.

The one adult contribution to "Family Chatter" is from a Mass with sermon given by Monsignor Uncle Joe Truxaw, a longtime pastor at Immaculate Conception Church in Los Angeles. Uncle Joe's church broadcasted Sunday morning Mass, and one Sunday Daddy pushed the record button. There's also news from KFWB and music from Frank Sinatra and Henry Mancini. Plates knocking and scraping, doors closing. It's an accurate sampling of the din, the commotion, including the random and rare quiet spaces.

The audio recording (which you can listen to on my website www.forgivemess.com) isn't the whole story of our collective life on Janss Way. We practiced piano and sports, baseball in the cul-de-sac, football in the backyard, basketball beneath the hoop where the driveway ended at the garage. We sewed and cooked and studied and squabbled. In the summer we went to the beach and some of the time stayed at the beach house.

We didn't watch much TV. At first there was one small screen shared by all of us. My first recollection of television was seeing the 1952 Democratic National Convention with Adlai Stevenson signs swinging above crowds of people—and the presidential nominee's eloquent voice. I was five years old. TV was all black-and-white then, and ours sat in a blond cabinet with folding doors. Mom limited the hours we could watch. The TV, a Sylvania, was in the family room, along with a turquoise-ish sofa across from a built-in brick fireplace. We used the fireplace even less than the television; it was a repository for newspapers and magazines, and perhaps even some of the McCall and Butterick dress and shirt patterns we older girls and Mom used with the sewing machine.

The dining room table was parked under windows that faced the backyard and a far fence covered in passion vine and bottlebrush; the table, usually folded, could be opened and leaves added for special occasions and celebrations. There was a rug on the floor. I can't visualize it, but it was comfortable enough if we wanted to watch TV and the few places on the couch were already taken. I recall being stretched out on the floor, leaning against the sofa, while watching the convention. There was an orange-hued Naugahyde chair with a matching ottoman that Daddy used, and of course some dining room chairs. If all ten of us were assembled, we managed to make it work. There were miserably sad days after the Kennedy assassination in November 1963 when we were glued to that television. I was a junior in high school the Sunday morning we saw and heard the gunshot that killed Lee Harvey Oswald. What a shock it was, watching the man accused of killing the president gunned down on live television.

Overall, we were happy at Janss Way. We made lots of good noise. At dinner we gathered at the built-in Formica table that straddled the boundary where the kitchen met the family room. As I've mentioned, we sat on benches, girls on one side, boys on the other. Sometimes Paul would eat at the breadboard. Once Michael was out of a highchair, four kids sat on each bench with our parents sitting in captain's chairs at the table's end. Mealtime was high energy and the food simple, typically meat and potatoes, mac and cheese, or creamed tuna on an English muffin.

There was so much to talk about, so many questions to ask. Teasing and silliness by Paul, and Maureen bossing us around. Mom was in charge, though, always at the head of the table. After dinner, the four oldest had jobs that rotated weekly. Rinsing off and washing up and loading the dishwasher, or wiping off and sweeping out. Eventually the younger kids had to take over.

Mom in her power place. Undated.

Daddy would come in late from work, still wearing his white pharmacy jacket, the top unsnapped. His eyes would look a bit dazed and tired behind thick glasses. "Hello, Patricia; hello, children," he'd say, giving Mom a quick kiss on the cheek. His dinner would be sitting on the stove atop a pan of water where Mom kept it warm. Then, walking with a slight limp, he'd cross through the kitchen to the hallway. It might be eight thirty or nine o'clock, and we would be finishing homework at the cleared table, or maybe watching the sliver of weekly TV allowed. Television created another opportunity for squabbles, compromise, blaming, and mediation by Mom—and Daddy, too, if the transgression was bad enough to require both parents.

"The boys always get to watch what they want."

"Be quiet, I can't hear what they're saying."

"Turn it down, it's too loud."

"He won't stop teasing me."

In retrospect, it was generally good-natured ribbing.

The noise dispersed as we headed to our rooms. The addition of a new bathroom and a large bedroom for the boys around 1964 decreased the overall bedtime tension. We'd go to sleep shouting good night across the bedrooms, from boys to girls, or girls to boys.

"Good night, Maureen."

"Good night, Bobby."

"Good night, Patsy."

"Good night, Paul."

And on through Evie, Johnny, Marguerite, and Michael. Most nights, Mom made the rounds to tuck us in and kiss us good night. She'd remind us to say our prayers. Even though she must've been exhausted, her attention at bedtime felt specific and loving. Jokers like Paul might shout "Good night, Pattycake" to me or "Good night, Hazelnut" to Evie. (Paul was a tease and Evie, the next in line after him in birth order, was often a target. He was thrilled when he discovered Evelyn, her full name, meant "hazelnut." That moniker endured much longer than Evie would have liked.) Peace descended upon the house when this good-night ritual was complete, the only sound the distant conversation of our parents, Daddy's sonorous timber and Mom's reassuring lilt. If Mom's nightly ritual was taking a bath, Daddy's retreat was to the back bathroom, the one off the back porch, where he'd set the newspaper on a basket of laundry as he settled onto the toilet.

There were aberrations of course, but the routines were soothing relief from the hubbub of daytime. Considering the chaos of the crowd, our lives and days were orderly and predictable. Yes, there were upheavals and meltdowns. I'll never forget when Paul circled the kitchen, family room, and living room in undies, screaming and chanting "Hog, pig, boar, meatloaf! Hog, pig, boar, meatloaf!" He hated meatloaf, everyone else's favorite, and when we had it, Mom reluctantly fed him a separate meal on the breadboard. Cries of "Shut up, Paul! You're crazy" met with "Don't say shut up" from Mom. "Shut up" was on her list of forbidden words and phrases, along with "damn," "hell," "shit," "fart," and a few other four- and five- and seven-letter words. I think I was in my fifties when I heard Mom utter "shit" for the first time.

I gained a few privileges as I got older and started staying up later to sew in the family room while watching Johnny Carson. I loved that alone time in the house with the sound of coughs and snores in the distance. I didn't have to say a word. Mom would usually be taking a bath, and she'd come out ready for bed to wish me good night, her voice muted by the hour and the size of her audience. Just me.

"Don't stay up too late," she'd say and kiss me good night. Mom had the final word.

Second Christmas After

Bam! A hand slaps down hard, displacing the delicate equilibrium of the extended Christmas dining table, unsettling the good china and wine glasses as it tilts toward my father's lap.

"You children stop this right now," he says. "You're out of line. Acting like alcoholics. You have no respect or control."

"Blah blah blah" is what most of us children hear. We were enjoying a cigar after dinner. It had been a heartbreaking and miserable year for our parents, for all of us, adjusting to Bobby's absence.

On occasion after occasion after the accident, Daddy had stood and made tearful tributes to his first son and junior. Mom once put her hand out to him saying, "Oh, Bob, we all miss Bobby," as he sat down, tears streaming down his face. There are lots of occasions in a family as large as ours. No doubt it had been to ward off the pall cast by Daddy's heartfelt but mawkish tributes that we—"we" being the seven surviving siblings, ages ten to twenty-four—had passed cigars around after dessert on this Christmas in 1970, and then spontaneously began raising glasses with our own toasts. Was I the ringleader? Probably. Second eldest. Opinionated, angry.

How patient did we have to be with his grief? With their grief? We'd been there for them. I'd shown up at home more often. But what about our grief? What about *my* grief? In that house, at that time, it seemed there was no room for anyone else's kicked heart but our parents'.

Our saluting took on a life of its own. Some of our toasts were silly, a few were serious, and then irreverent escalated to profane: tributes to Jimi Hendrix, to Gomer Pyle, to Miss Roche (a teacher at the all-boys Catholic school ridiculed by her students), to Ho Chi Minh, to Jane Fonda, to Father Quatannens. Of course we were drinking. Auntie Maureen, our proper auntie, a probation officer and the one to stay home and care for her mother, Nana Sweeney, kept pace at first. We started adding f-bombs: to the fucking war, to Nixon and Kissinger, to our fucking Republican cousins, to Uncle Neil, to Omar, one of our many runaway dogs. To the Chicago Seven. It was such a relief.

"You children are so disrespectful," Auntie Maureen suddenly scolds, validating Daddy's reprimands. "This is no way to be carrying on. You have no manners. Patricia, how can you let your children get away with this?" Her irritation is keen, her pale middle-aged face taut, arched in disapproval. She pushes a hand against her dyed black hair. It doesn't move. Most everyone at the table sucks in breath, waits for what will come next.

"We're just having fun," someone exhales, biting a trembling lip, struggling not to smirk or laugh.

Mom, who'd been toying with a cigar and even briefly put it between her lips, sets the cigar down. "They're just having a good time together, Maureen. Just having some fun. They don't mean any harm," she says.

Mom cheerfully explains this to her older sister, the one she'd most wanted to be like. The one she'd skipped eighth grade to follow to high school a year early. But Aunt Maureen remains so incensed that Patricia, our mother, must decide whether to stand by her sister or her children. Mom has an inscrutable smile and does not take sides. She's changed since losing Bobby; she pauses now before making snap judgments. If she waits it out, maybe she won't have to commit to a course of action. Maybe Daddy will step in. Her childless sister cannot possibly understand what this family's been through.

Usually when we'd get something derisive going, mocking an uncle or aunt, local personage or politician, or even an absent sibling, Mom would at some point interrupt and say, "Oh, children, you shouldn't talk like that." But most often it was with a laugh and a smile. I believe she enjoyed our repartee and bonding.

Contrary to his usual deference to his wife, Daddy takes a stand this time. As his hand slaps down on the table again, Mom's eyes widen. Her hand goes horizontal across her mouth, a default gesture intended to look gracious but triggered by discomfort. Aunt Maureen jerks up and steps away from her chair. She announces she's leaving.

"Thanks for the dinner, Patricia and Bob," she says, scanning the table with her dark eyes. "I think I'll let you resolve this yourselves."

"Now calm down, Maureen, please," Mother entreats. "Don't ruin our Christmas. Please."

"We were just fooling around," Maureen, my sister and Aunt Maureen's namesake, says. "Nobody wanted to offend you." Aunt Maureen shakes her head at our sister and all of us, clearly not amused.

"I've seen enough, Patricia. Merry Christmas indeed," she says, backing away from the crowded table. She grabs her purse and coat from the living room and bolts out of the house. Somewhere between the front door and the driveway, she misses a step and falls on the pavement.

"You children are monsters. Now look what you've done to your Aunt Maureen!" Daddy grumbles as he makes his way to the porch. He sees what appears to be blood and rushes to help his injured sister-in-law.

Older and younger kids huddle as an organic unit. Is she really bleeding? At most it's a scrape. Mom is at the door, hands clasped in quasi prayer position, silent, distraught. This Christmas has turned into a disaster. The septet of siblings retreats to the table, whispering with some stifled sniggering. Oh, schadenfreude. Then the eldest sibling, the younger Maureen, giggles nervously and says she feels bad for poor Auntie Maureen. She suggests maybe we went too far, thus separating herself from the rest of the clique. It was our sister Maureen's unlucky fate to play the sibling scold, which sometimes alienated her from our fraternal federation.

I cannot imagine why Daddy let Aunt Maureen drive herself home as inebriated, angry, and wounded as she was, but that was in the days before designated drivers, and Daddy had become quite undone. The emotion of a big holiday without his oldest son had ruptured his equable container. Here was our father aggrieved. After scooping her into her Impala and watching her drive out of the cul-de-sac, he came back inside, righteous, huffing, steaming mad. He proceeded to remove all the wine bottles from the table, and then he moved to the cupboard above the refrigerator, the location of his drugstore and liquor cabinet. Daddy was a pharmacist who suffered from chronic pain. He self-medicated. But the alcohol, not the drugs, was his objective.

"Hey Daddy, Auntie Maureen was drinking too," I remind him.

"Yeah, what's wrong with her, anyhow?" Evie chimes in.

"Maybe she's a Republican," Paul quips.

"If you don't watch out, you'll become just like your Aunt Edna, Patsy," Daddy says. "You're all drinking way too much. I'm getting rid of it. Right now. You should try to be a better example."

Daddy's Aunt Edna, Nana Truxaw's younger sister, was a sweetheart of a great-aunt who sewed stylish outfits for my Toni doll. She had a "drinking problem," and on occasion, Daddy had to go pick Edna up off her floor.

The cluster of us watched, subdued and horrified, as he dumped all the booze down the drain. Daddy didn't keep a vast supply of liquor, but whatever was there—bourbon, an old bottle of Irish whiskey, brandy—down and away it went. We siblings did the dishes and cleaned up. Mom went to lie down. In 2023, a photo of Michael from that day surfaced among a batch of old negatives Johnny had been scanning. Michael wears a smart-alecky expression and holds a stogie in his mouth.

Christmas Day. Top row, from left: Johnny, Mom, Evie, Paul, me, and Daddy; bottom row, from left: Michael, Maureen, and Marguerite. 1969 or 1970.

I remember picking up holiday debris later that night, or maybe it was the next day. Grabbing Bobby's empty stocking, I heard and felt the crinkle of paper inside. It was a short note in Daddy's distinct scribble; he'd written to tell Bobby how much he was missed. Fifteen months since the accident and we siblings were back to our group antics. We'd been hard on Daddy, and I felt mean and sad as I slipped the letter back into the stocking. His grief grabbed my throat and chest. I had no remedy to offer and was relieved to be heading back to DC in a few days.

It's a pity we were ignorant about grief counseling then.

Daddy: Dearest Wandering Boy

Daddy in Morro Bay, CA, probably making breakfast. Undated.

I don't want you to have the impression Daddy was always the grieving, disappointed man who caused us kids to cringe as he rose to toast Bobby. Less than a year after Bobby's death, Daddy spontaneously hopped on an airplane to help move his second-eldest daughter, me, from Anaheim to Washington, DC, for my first postcollege job. We chatted as we crossed the country, shared drinks and the view. At the time, I felt stunned and dismayed by Daddy's gesture. I'd had my own plan for the five-hour transition from Orange County to DC, and at age twenty-three, it didn't include making nice conversation with my dad. Later, I'd wish I'd made better use of the opportunity. I didn't realize at the time how many questions went unasked and unanswered; how much more I'd want to know about my father.

Daddy took the next return flight home when we got to DC, spending the better part of the day aloft. For his part, he was disappointed a later cross-country flight wasn't available. He'd hoped to deliver me to the apartment I'd be sharing with my old friend Amanda and a new friend, Linda, both colleagues at the United States Student Press Association. Instead, he never left Dulles International Airport, and Paul and Johnny had to make their second trip of the day from Anaheim to Los Angeles International Airport (LAX) to pick up our chagrined but smiling father late that night.

Daddy loved to travel. His mom, our Nana Truxaw, mother of eight, was an artist, poet, volunteer, and gadabout. Married to a busy country doctor, she managed their property and home and eagerly drove all over California and beyond—to Los Angeles, Fresno, San Francisco—usually to see distant relatives, frequently taking some of her kids along. She was a whirlwind of industry and inspiration to Daddy and all of us. She took Maureen and me to the Seattle World's Fair in 1962, I crossed the Golden Gate Bridge for the first time with Nana. But I'm getting off track.

In September 1936, when he was seventeen, Daddy and his younger brother Joe were moving a table for a neighbor out to Placentia, which back then was in the countryside five or six miles from Anaheim. He drove a new truck, about which Nana Truxaw wrote, "Bob was quite proud." When the table started to slide around the bed of the truck, Daddy pulled to the side of the road to secure it. A reckless driver going the opposite direction struck him as he stood on the street side of the truck's running board. The impact projected him twenty feet up and over the truck. He landed hard on the dusty shoulder. His brother was unhurt.

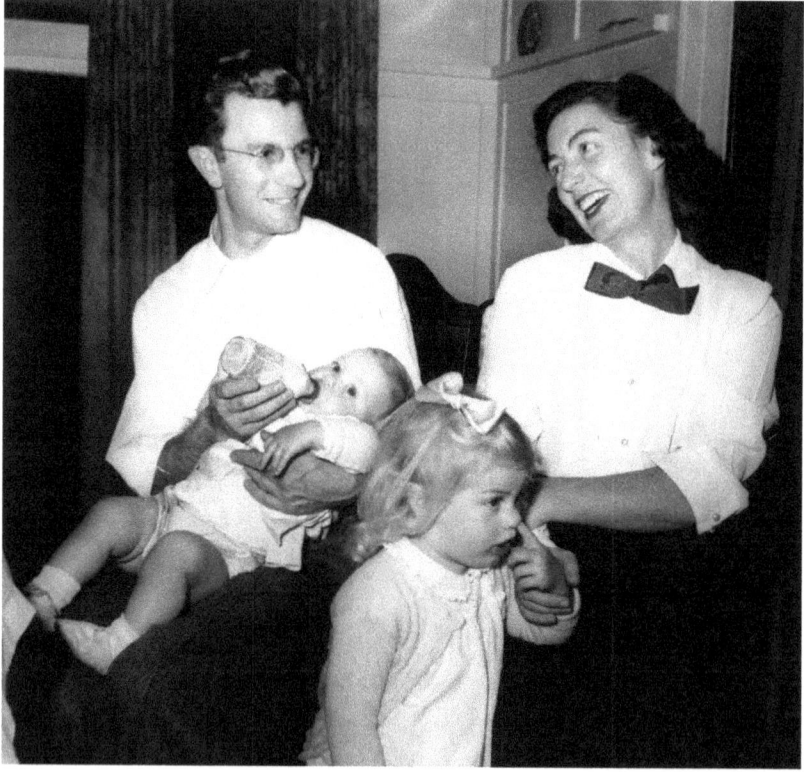

Daddy, Baby Paul, me, and Mom. Late 1940s.

As Nana describes in her *Story of Dr. John,*[1] "He was taken to Anaheim General Hospital where no one knew who he was so the doctor cupped his hand and called into the ear of the broken body,

'Who are you? What is your name?'

Bob answered very pleadingly from his subconscious mind, 'Bob, Bob.'

The doctor called into the ear, 'Bob who?'

That was the last conscious thought Bob had for almost a week," Nana wrote.

The doctor on call was John W. Truxaw, MD, who realized with a jolt that the injured youth was his second son. He called for a priest, and they took Daddy directly to the operating room. He had a broken nose, seven broken ribs, and a leg broken in three places. He took up knitting while recovering in the hospital. As a kid hearing this story, I visualized my grown dad sitting in bed, smiling and knitting, a sweet detail. He'd lain on an uncomfortable fracture bed, receiving care from many of Grampa-Dad's medical friends. He'd endured a lengthy and painful recuperation. His senior year of high school was delayed, and so was the start of college. Daddy had a bum leg for the rest of his days.

Daddy had planned to be a doctor like Grampa-Dad, to head to premed courses after a year of college. But the accident, and then the impending World War II, interfered with his studies and career plans. (Thirty-two years later, in another September, Bob Truxaw Jr., my brother who had similar career plans, was in an accident that was fatal.)

In the summer of 1937, after missing most of the prior school year, Daddy was well enough to take a long train trip by himself from Anaheim to Iowa and Nebraska, visiting Chicago and relatives along the way. He kept a diary and wrote frequent letters. When we were looking through boxes and family history after

---

1   The *Story of Dr. John* is a biography of our grandfather, John W. Truxaw, that Nana wrote for the family.

Mom died, some of the felicitous finds included correspondence between Daddy and his parents, such as frequent, warm newsy letters from Nana Truxaw, glad to hear Daddy was doing well and probably gaining weight. There was also a gem from Grampa-Dad written on several sheets of prescription pad paper, dated "June 26, '37 1:30 a.m. Sat" and addressed to "Dearest Wandering Boy." Grampa-Dad had completed his quickly written note in two sittings because:

Monday 12:40 a.m. Well Dear Bob you can see what a time I have trying to write a little letter—the other night on Sat a.m. had a fellow all cut up in a wreck and it was about daylight when I got thru and too late to finish any letter.

The prescription pad jottings, a father grabbing time to "write a little letter" to his "Dearest Wandering Boy" creates an apt handle for our fidgety, curious, wise, whimsical father who treasured travel and was himself a letter writer. It's a gratifying lens through which to view Daddy, and for that, I'm grateful to a grandfather whose countenance I only dimly recall.

Grampa-Dad, as we called him, was a craggy-faced, kind man whose home office was between the back porch and dining room at The Old Place, the large, elegant house at 887 Los Angeles Street with its orange groves, chickens, cow, barn, and more. Daddy and his seven siblings were raised there, and our nuclear family had the good fortune of living there while waiting for Janss Way to be built in the early 1950s. By then the chickens and cows were long gone. It was an enchanting and at times scary place for a second grader: lots of space, nooks, and crannies for games and hiding. The attic had a picture of Jesus, I think with a crown of thorns, and his eyes opened and closed. It gave me the shivers.

Grampa-Dad died in 1952 when I was five. I remember Daddy flying off to Iowa, where Grampa-Dad had been visiting family and died. ("My dad is sick" is how he put it to us kids.) When Daddy returned, I rode with Mom to pick him up at the rural airport on MacArthur Boulevard near what's UC Irvine and John Wayne Airport today. Nana Truxaw, Grampa-Dad's wife, died a few months after Bobby in November 1969. By then she'd moved to a house just blocks from us on Janss Street (not to be confused with Janss Way).

Today The Old Place is a restaurant called The Anaheim White House. The Truxaw family gathers there once a year for a Christmas reunion, always noting a plaque on the wall that commemorates its history and Dr. Truxaw, who was on call twenty-four hours a day, treating rich or poor in and around Anaheim. The Truxaw clan is delighted that the owner of the restaurant, Bruno Serato, carries on the tradition of service in his own way today by feeding hungry children—a service for which he was recognized as a CNN Hero in 2011.[2]

Maybe because his "bum leg," as he termed it, never stopped bothering him, Daddy was most happy on the move, whether by car, air, or railroad. I have photos of him as a young man on the road in Idaho and Mexico, shirtless and handsome in some of them. He kept a diary prior to and during World War II wherein he writes about frequent drives from Anaheim into Los Angeles, and about attending pharmacy school for a while in Seattle. His letters home describe visits around Washington state and beyond. He attended four colleges before finally getting his degree. Despite working long hours as a pharmacist, a profession that required him to stand all day, he found time to plan and get his wife and children, sometimes all eight of us, out of town. We went to the desert, the mountains, the beach, the Kern River, Palm Springs, and a dude ranch in Twentynine Palms where we had an unforgettable adventure on horses. One Friday night in Las Vegas, Mom

---

2   "Sir Bruno Serato," Chef Bruno Serato, accessed February 15, 2025, https://www.chefbrunoserato.com/about/.

and Daddy stuck us kids in a hot motel room with a crying baby Michael so they could go out to a casino, whether to see a show or gamble I don't recall—most likely just to get a few hours free from the rest of us. They were so late in returning that we older kids worried they weren't coming back.

A few weeks after his trek to DC with me, Daddy wrote me a letter that begins, "Dear Fellow Traveler." He's sorry he didn't have time to visit the nation's capital, he writes, but "I've done it again." "It" was taking Mom, Michael, Marguerite, Johnny, and Evie to Hawaii. The letter describes the Hawaiian adventure in specifics: a disappointing Honolulu, a second flight to Maui, the drive to Hana, a further flight to the Big Island, waterfalls, beaches. A subsequent letter from Mom corroborates "the beautiful and surprising trip."

I've had mixed feelings about Daddy over the years. Yes, he could be maudlin. I came to dread his tears and tributes to Bobby. Yet, he was clearly and deservedly bereft when Bobby was suddenly gone. It was a huge loss for all of us, but Bobby was and would always be the first and only Robert J. Truxaw Jr. That he died too soon—that is, a day after his twenty-first birthday—is indisputable. How to deal with this loss, how we as a family dealt with it, is another matter that those of us still alive continue to discuss more than fifty years later.

It was a hard time to be at home. I wasn't there and was glad of it. I know it was hard because over the years I've heard about the toll it took on those left behind at Janss Way to live with the reminders of Bobby's absence: his schoolbooks, letters, windbreaker, button-down shirts, and more. Hard, too, to live so close to extended family members—the nanas, aunts and uncles, sisters and brothers—who didn't know how to talk to Mom or Daddy, how to share an impossible loss.

The boys, my four brothers, each had a corner with a desk, a chest of drawers, and a chair in that one large room that had been added on to the house. There were baseball mitts, bats, footballs, team pennants, bulletin boards. Bobby lived in a dorm at UCLA the last year of his life but had been home for the summer, working at Disneyland, going to the beach, visiting Sue in Bakersfield, and joking around with his roommate-brothers Paul, Johnny, and Michael.

Thoughtful, pensive: Johnny, Paul, Daddy, and Michael with picture of Bobby on the tabletop at Janss Way. Reflection of unknown photographer in the background. 1970.

I didn't wonder at the time what it was like to live in the boys' room, or at least I didn't want to dwell on it. I do recall visiting Janss Way one night not too long after the accident. Sitting on the kitchen side of the Formica table after dinner, I heard the front door open and close with a *whoosh*. But no one was there. A shudder of hollowness caught me off guard. Was Bobby still around, somewhere?

I see now that Daddy's remedy for helping his wife and children, and probably himself, was to get everyone out of town and away from the house and the physical symbols of Bobby's absence. The need to be elsewhere eventually propelled my parents to leave Janss Way and move from Anaheim up the coast to Morro Bay. As I pore over letters and photos and sit with Daddy's spirit while writing this book, my memories and view of a whole man fill out, with appreciation and some regret. I understand now that there was something brave and escapist in his impetuous decision to shepherd me to my new life in DC. I didn't know what to make of him back then, and I wasn't curious. Maybe I only *thought* he was disappointed never to have made it to medical school.

Two weeks after the Hawaii trip, Daddy got a last-minute flight to Kansas to attend his nephew Patrick Sweeney's wedding. Pat was one of the tight trio of cousins—Patrick, Tim, and Bobby—who were all born in 1948 and who formed a collective unit through their grammar school years at St. Boniface and on into high school. It was an impulsive move on Daddy's part. The sister of the groom later said how delighted they all were to see Uncle Bob dashing into the church at the last minute. I believe Daddy went to Pat's wedding for Bobby.

After the Kansas wedding trip, Daddy settled into work and helped Mom plan for Paul and Maureen's weddings. He worked as a pharmacist at SupeRX Drug Store, a quick drive from home, though sometimes he walked the half mile. In my imagination, he started walking instead of driving for the private time it gave him to talk to God and Bobby.

And then, in 1973, Daddy instigated the best getaway ever. With help from a small financial settlement over Bobby's death, he meticulously planned an almost month-long trip to Ireland for any family member available to go.

Daddy isn't of Irish descent; Truxa (the original spelling) is of Czechoslovakian origin. No, this was a trip to Mom's family's motherland. For Daddy, it was a once-in-a-lifetime wander to a somewhat mysterious and mythical country. The prospect of leprechauns appealed to his whimsical side—much later he would write a never-published children's story called "Grinky and the Groudlins" about magical, leprechaun-like characters.

I lived in DC in May of 1973 and was up for a trip. A recent relationship had concluded poorly, and the Vietnam War and my job were coming to an end. I arranged to rendezvous with the rest of the family at John F. Kennedy International Airport (JFK) in New York City for the flight to Shannon, Ireland. When lightning lit up the New York sky, however, things didn't go as planned. My short flight from DC to New York circled the airport, unable to make a safe landing, and the pilot considered heading to Newark; unbeknownst to me, the California Truxaws were doing the same at the tail end of their flight from Los Angeles. Electrical storms caused delayed landings, frayed nerves, and missed flights. This was way before cell phones, the notion of texting only in science fiction or a laboratory, about as likely as a pot of gold.

My plane landed eventually, but not before our ticketed TWA flight had departed for Ireland. *What if they left without me?* Probably thanks to a white courtesy telephone, I managed to locate my family in the international terminal. It felt like a miracle. As we gathered, I learned Daddy had succeeded in getting all seven of us seats on a later Aer Lingus flight. How ironic it would've been, we joked later, if we'd all died in separate plane crashes. We'd had plenty of time that day to contemplate such an ending to the trip and our family. Michael, then just twelve years old, was terrified and shaken up by the scary conclusion to his first-ever flight, but Daddy was elated. He was jacked. It was like he'd been plugged in and was sparking.

My memory sees us inside a wide Aer Lingus plane with a lounge space where we were able to relax and laugh as stewardesses tempted us with tastes of Guinness, Irish Mist, and Irish whiskey. Such was the start of our trip to Ireland. It was with great ease, and dare I say joy, that I took my place among the family. Yet another electrical connection tethered us to one another, enduring for the next several weeks and beyond.

Except for Mom, who'd been to Ireland as a child, it was the first time any of us had been overseas. It felt supercharged, new, curious, quaint, delightful. We romped in fields and shot a silly film, playful and exhilarated. I turned twenty-six during this trip, though in photos I appear much younger. We all do. Looking at film and snapshots fifty years later, I see my parents in their fifties: Daddy in his reddish plaid coat, playful; Mom, silly and pretty, relaxed. Evie, twenty-one, wearing long dark braids. Marguerite, sixteen, blonde, pretty, sturdy, and playing soccer with Michael, slightly pudgy at twelve. Johnny, twenty, his hair wild and full and browner than I remember, curious about everything. Many of us wear Aran sweaters as we walk, play, and explore. Michael wears a traditional Irish wool hat. I explore Blarney Castle in an orange and purple plaid cape. Yes, we all kissed the Blarney Stone and remarked at the billboards: "Keep Ireland Tidy" and "Guinness is Good for You." We were lighthearted, at least until we arrived in the North.

We'd intended to stay with Mom's cousin James Doherty and his large family in Derry, the birthplace of Nana Sweeney and an aunt and uncle. The night before our arrival, however, a car bomb had detonated across from their home, so James booked us at an inn over the border in Greencastle in nearby County Donegal. It was June 1973. We were entering a war zone, and it felt like it. Rolled barbed wire and armed British soldiers at a checkpoint. Machine gun–bearing military personnel standing outside the car while we awaited a possible pat down. British Royal Military Police (RMPs) searching cars and demanding to see identification. We all remained very quiet. When I was in Derry forty-six years later, in 2019, crossing the border to Donegal was a completely unremarkable experience and part of an evening dinner out or a Saturday afternoon trip to an art gallery. But back then, it was a place of unease and danger.

We learned so much from James and his wife, his sister-in-law, and his nine children. For one thing, the adults drank a lot. For another, James and others in his family were well-versed in Irish and English history, and even in American and world history. Also, it wasn't uncommon for a bomb to be discovered in the dressing room of a department store while one of our teenage cousins was out shopping. (The next chapter of this book, "The Irish Connection," contains more details about our Irish family.) Our notion of family expanded to this other continent, as did our understanding of democracy, civil rights, repression, fear, and courage.

We spent our final night in Ireland at Bunratty Castle, enjoying a traditional Irish feast where the alcohol flowed. Michael recalls investigating with Daddy beyond the roped-off areas of the castle and noticing Daddy was tipsy. For some reason this information makes me very happy. Our father was letting go; good for him.

Daddy pulled it off. Even though he stayed in the background a good deal of the time, the wandering boy got his family on a grand and mind-altering adventure. This was the longest period I'd spent with the family since moving to DC, and every minute of the trip was infused with the energy we felt at the outset. Even our time in Northern Ireland was adrenaline-charged in its newness and lessons. The trip served as a nice family reset before my return to California and Janss Way two months later to begin the next stage of my life.

Bunratty Castle, Ireland. Top row, from left: waitstaff, Johnny, Michael, and waitstaff; bottom row, from left: Mom, Daddy, me, and Marguerite. June 1973.

Ireland was not Daddy's last trip, of course. When Michael and Marguerite were the only kids at home, the four of them went to the desert, the mountains, the Olympic Peninsula, and more. Later Mom and Daddy traveled to the East Coast, and Daddy finally got to visit Washington, DC, properly.

In addition to chronic pain in his leg, later in life Daddy suffered the effects of a spinal fracture he sustained while serving as a pallbearer at Auntie Maureen's funeral in 1989. This injury led to discovering his osteoporosis. His skeleton shrunk in a few years' time. Daddy took his final voyage—a drive in the middle of the night—about a year prior to his death from complications related to osteoporosis. While my mother slept, he went out to the garage wearing a nightshirt covered with baseball players, got himself positioned in the Buick, pushed the garage door opener, and backed out the car. He'd lost more than a foot in height by this time. His osteoporosis was so bad you could put a tray on his back to transport drinks from the kitchen to the living room. He had a mustache that made him look slightly naughty.

I imagine Daddy sighed with relief when he reached the coast highway a block from the house. The road stretched both north and south indefinitely. He knew he was in for a long ride in the dark if he went north: After Morro Bay would come Cayucos, and then little of note until Cambria, and then nothing for at least one hundred miles. He headed south. He wasn't properly dressed. He didn't have his wallet. His body was crooked. He was probably on too many medications to pass a drug test. His elation throttled back by the reality of what he'd done, he never made it out of town; he exited Highway 1 at Main Street and drove around Morro Bay until police lights flashed behind him. They called Mom and drove him home.

Daddy may have been disappointed at his capture, but I recall his talking about the episode with pride and glee. "I just wanted to go for a drive," he explained.

The Irish Connection

The earliest picture I have of Mom is one taken in Ireland when she was quite young. She's standing with her father and her older siblings, Kevin, Evie, and Maureen. They wear shirts that have an *M* on the front, which no doubt stands for Moville, a beach in Ireland Mom used to talk about and one we visited in 1973. The photo was probably taken in 1920 or soon thereafter. Mom looks to be about four years old. A cap shades her face, and I see little that resembles the features of my future mother.

The others are more visible and identifiable. Evie, the eldest, stands ramrod straight, a portrait of good posture and assuredness. She must have been about eight. Maureen's long dark bangs don't conceal familiar dark eyes. She was a year older than Mom, so would have been around five. Kevin has the rascally look of a seven-year-old boy impatient to get the picture-taking over. Finally, there's our grandfather Patrick who stands behind his children, darkly handsome, in his early thirties. I've treasured this photo because I never met him and because I catch fresh glimpses of siblings and cousins in all the faces every time I look at it.

Grandfather Sweeney in Moville, County Donegal, Ireland, with (from left) Kevin, Mom, Maureen, and Evie. Around 1920.

Although born in Stockton, California, Mom spent part of her childhood in Derry, Northern Ireland, after her parents, Patrick (P. J.) and Mary Angela (Minnie) Devlin Sweeney, returned to their home country in 1920 with the first four of their eventual eight children. The early story of the P. J. Sweeneys is marked by the peripatetic wandering characteristic of immigrants during and between world events. They were often on the move, looking for the best place to settle with their young family.

Mom spoke dreamily about her childhood in and around Derry, and often about her father. "Oh children," she'd say. "Daddy was so handsome." And so he is in photos, tall, dark, intense, and yes, handsome. She reminisced nostalgically about the beach in Moville where they'd go to swim, and about a grand house that had a ballroom.

We relished hearing stories about Nana and Grandfather Sweeney's early life and romantic courtship. Mom told us that Nana and her sister Sara fell out of communication over a man, that man being our Grandfather Sweeney. I learned more about the family intrigue in 2019 when I visited Derry with my niece Annie, the daughter of my sister, Maureen. A love triangle, a secret wedding, an escape to New Zealand, bad blood! Here's what I learned over tea in our second cousin Ian Doherty's kitchen:

Our mild-mannered Nana and the grandfather we never met, P. J. Sweeney, dramatically fled Ireland for New Zealand in 1910. Auntie Evie was born there in 1911. Nana's sister Sara, who'd been in love with P. J., eventually married Thomas Doherty. They had one child, James Doherty, the one who took such good care of us when we visited Ireland in 1973. Ian Doherty, the cousin who gave me all this information over tea, is James's son and Sara's grandson. Their mothers being sisters, James and Mom were first cousins. But as their mothers were estranged, James and Mom never met until the 1960s. The oldest American Sweeney, my generation's Bill LeVecke, is the one who ended the decades-long family stand-off when he charmed his way into meeting the Dohertys during a college graduation trip. There was a flurry of activity and travel between California and Derry after Bill's breakthrough, and the families have stayed in touch for sixty years and counting.

Nana and Grandfather Sweeney spent those early years in New Zealand; then moved to the United States, where Mom was born; then went back to Ireland, where Auntie Milo and Uncle Noel were born, their fifth and sixth children. They eventually made their way back to the United States, where they stayed. They ventured first to St. Petersburg, Florida, and then to Quincy, Massachusetts. They had two more children, Ailish and Joyce. In 1928, Grandfather Sweeney drove his large family across the country in a Phaeton, settling in Anaheim. By then he'd worked as an entrepreneur and a builder. His final job was as a salesman. "Daddy could sell anything," Mom told us with pride.

Grandfather Sweeney died young, at age forty-eight, during the Depression in 1935. He left behind Nana Sweeney and six girls and two boys. It was a shattering blow. The four eldest, including Mom, scuttled education and career plans and pitched in to support the family. Mom got a job working at the phone company. In 1940, they were able to buy a house on West Street in Anaheim. Evie, Kevin, Maureen, and Patricia (Mom), the four in the photo with Grandfather Sweeney, are listed on the grant deed as joint tenants. Mom was close with all her siblings and always said her sisters were her best friends.

Nana never became an American citizen. She had a green card, which made her a lawful permanent resident. She spoke with a soft brogue, her words wrapped in a whisper. She never appeared to be a woman with a dramatic or even troubled history. It was hard to imagine that she'd once been a teacher who drove a trap—a light two-wheeled carriage pulled by a horse or pony—to work. As children we spent many hours in Nana Sweeney's kitchen, on her lanai, and in her yard. To us, to me, she made the best peanut butter cookies in the world.

In 2023, a cousin informed me that Grandfather Sweeney had

died of cirrhosis of the liver. It must have been awful to live with an unemployed drinker during the Depression, this cousin said. The death certificate I have, signed by our other grandfather, Dr. John W. Truxaw, lists the cause of death as cerebral hemorrhage due to chronic parenchymatous nephritis. This translates to kidney death, which is often related to excessive alcohol consumption. So, Grampa-Dad Truxaw, Daddy's father, signed the death certificate for Mom's father. Far as I know, our parents weren't friends back then, but they may have been acquainted or had some connection through siblings who attended the same church or high school. Indeed, Daddy's sister Mary Ellen and Mom were friends in high school—that's how Mom and Daddy met.

"Daddy died of a stroke" is how Mom always explained her father's death. I don't know if she ever read his death certificate, but she never once said a word about his alcohol consumption, just that he'd had a bad stomach. "That's where you get your poor stomach, Patsy," she'd tell me. It turns out a bad stomach isn't the only thing I inherited from the good-looking grandfather I never met.

Would it have made a difference for my generation of Sweeneys if our genetic heritage hadn't been hidden from us? At least two of our cousins have died alcohol-related deaths, and who knows how many others are affected. That's not even counting our Irish cousins, the children of Mom's cousin James, among whom several have lost their lives or been otherwise impacted by the diseases of alcoholism and addiction.

Many causes may contribute to the keeping of family secrets, not all of them nefarious. Immigration, the Depression, socioeconomics, religious and cultural biases—all of these likely played a role in my family's drive to maintain appearances and look away from hard truths. I must wonder, though, who among us would have lived longer or stopped indulging sooner, instead of yielding to booze's ruinous self-destructive properties, had the predisposition to alcoholism in our family been faced more openly.

Patsy: Magic Dress

Outlier

It's 1968 and I'm sitting on the stoop of my small alley rental house in Newport Beach, smogged in turbulence. I've dropped out of school for the winter quarter; I've recently defied Mom and paid the price. Before I know it I'm off the stoop and headed toward Ventura in my yellow Ford Fairlane, the one Uncle Jerry found for me. But my memory is correcting itself as I write. I might be driving south to Oceanside, not north to Ventura. Memory fog permeates the past. I'm driving up or down the coast trying to figure things out. The light is the peculiar winter beach light, a watery yellow gray. I'm awash in it, in yellow gray. I'm not yet twenty-one. My brother is not yet dead. There's plenty of time to get it together.

I defied Mom by going to San Francisco with Amy and Amanda. She wouldn't give me her permission, let alone a blessing. We felt compelled to visit Haight-Ashbury. We had to see it, smell it, have it for ourselves. We drove in Amy's Valiant from late afternoon into the evening and night. Amy did most of the driving. I sat in the back, excited and worried. I saw a sign for King City and wondered whether we were getting close. It takes a lot out of me to openly defy Mom. She will not forget.

"If you go, don't expect any further help from me," she'd said.

I broke away—away from the claustrophobic Irish Catholic extended family, from Orange County, from being a good Catholic girl. The world around us was exploding. Vietnam, Buffalo Springfield, Nixon, Cesar Chavez, the Doors. Phil Pearlman, our neighbor and cohort at the student newspaper at UC Irvine, knew Big Brother and the Holding Company. Phil was always talking about Chet and Janis.[3] He did light shows, and Amanda and I helped sometimes, swirling glass plates of what looked like colored Jell-O atop an overhead projector. And the music—it was electrifying. This wasn't Marywood; this wasn't St. Boniface. It wasn't what any of us had expected, but it felt like the truth. Why should I feel bad about it?

I don't recall where we slept in San Francisco, but I have a picture of Amanda sitting on some steps in front of a Haight-Ashbury Victorian. She hides behind her purse, one hand extended above her head in a peace sign. We walked around, outsiders gawking. Stayed two nights and returned on a Sunday so we could make it to classes and work on Monday. We were still good girls. It was an innocent trip, before the drugs, before all that was yet to come. We were virgins in so many ways.

Mom was enraged by my defiance. I felt shunned by her and most of the family, seven brothers and sisters, my dad, the Sweeney cousins, Nana Sweeney, the aunties. *Patsy is going bad.* That was the message. *Patsy is hanging out with longhairs. Probably communists and drug addicts too.* My friends embarrassed and confused her. Nana Truxaw gave me ten dollars and said to go buy some potatoes.

---

3   Big Brother and the Holding Company was a band started by Chet Helms, considered the Father of San Francisco music. Janis Joplin was their lead singer until she left the band in 1968. Our editor and friend, Phil Pearlman, brought the group and others to UC Irvine and put on psychedelic light shows during the concerts.

I think Mom's view of me made me ill. It was called gastritis. My gut, my core, felt tangled up; it didn't easily adapt to the disfavor and void of Mom. She cut me off, so I requested extra hours at the campus library to cover rent.

And I decided to take this drive. It's one of the loneliest drives of my life. Who am I without them, without Mom's approval? Traveling in a new and shifting space, I see myself on the road: flannel shirt, shoulder-length hair, round wire-rimmed glasses. I'm not looking for answers so much as accommodating a metamorphosis, driving away from childhood into myself. I try to set Mom at a distance. I know I'll go back to school. I know the reach of my life is broadening, and I welcome it. It's scary and nerve-wracking and lonely, but I have no choice.

I stop somewhere after driving for about an hour. The yellow-gray late morning gives way to more clear coastal light. I stand outside the car and look at the ocean in Ventura. Or is it Oceanside? Both places are spokes on the new radius of my life. I'm stretching my distance, exercising my autonomy. Before the end of the year I'll see New York.

The Phone Call

"P. T., wake up. Wake up." Amy, a friend who'd graduated from UC Irvine, married, and moved to San Francisco stood over me, an apparition in a long nightgown. "Your father's on the phone. He wants to talk to you."

I'd been asleep on a hard floor in a round room. Warm lamps glowed outside the windows on Stanyan Street, backlighting Amy's waiflike form.

"What?" I asked, groggy after just a few hours' sleep. "My dad? Is on the phone? Did he say what it was?" My heartbeat quickened as I stumbled to the phone in the kitchen of Amy's San Francisco apartment. A greasy black clock read 2:34.

"Daddy? What's going on?" I whispered.

"There's been an accident. Bobby was in an accident, and you're not here. They took him to the hospital." His voice was thick, almost rough.

"What!" My grip on the phone tightened. "What? Is he . . ."

"His chest was crushed, and well, he didn't make it. We didn't get there in time." His voice cracked, and I visualized his prominent Adam's apple rise in his throat as he tried to swallow.

"What?" I asked again. "Didn't get there in time for what?"

My hand pressed against my chest as my head bent into the phone. "But I just saw him two days ago," I said. He'd come by my place on Balboa Peninsula.

"We couldn't find you anywhere, Patsy. Your brother is dead, and we had to track down Amanda to find where you were. Do you think you'll come home?" he pleaded.

I started to explain that Mom knew I was in San Francisco to cover the Regents meeting and visit friends.

"But I just saw him two days ago," I insisted. "I just saw him." He was in love. I held myself in a twist of disbelief.

"He was on his way to a football game with his friend, John. They got hit by a car."

"My God, Daddy. I'm so sorry. I'll be home soon as I can."

It was early morning on September 20, 1969. Amy and her husband got me to the airport for the first Air Cal flight back to Orange County. Paul met me at the airport. He was now the big brother.

Paul and me at Mom's burial at Holy Sepulcher Cemetery in Orange, CA. November 2014.

Bill's Wedding

Our cousin Bill LeVecke got married in early May of 1970, less than eight months after Bobby's accident. It was a huge event in our parish, family, and community. He married a Karcher, one of Carl Karcher's girls, Margaret. Carl was the founder and owner of Carl's Jr. The burgers. I don't remember whether the Karchers had twelve or fourteen children, but it was a lot. I'd gone to school with Carleen Karcher, who was a year younger than Margaret. Bill was the first Sweeney cousin, the first child of Auntie Milo and Uncle Neil, and the LeVeckes had a burgeoning liquor business. We joked that the Booze King was marrying the Burger Queen, but it would be more accurate to say they were the Prince and Princess of burgers and booze.

Not only was Carl, the patriarch, a self-made man, having gone from a burger cart to a successful fast-food chain that continued to expand for many years; he was also active and outspoken in Orange County politics. He was an avid supporter of John Schmitz, a John Bircher, who at the time of the wedding was a California state senator. Schmitz would be elected to the United States Congress in 1974 with the support, as his Wikipedia page says, "of fast-food magnate Carl Karcher."[4]

Bill wasn't a John Bircher far as I know, but he was a Goldwater supporter and a Republican through and through. I cut my political arguing teeth in dialogue and disputes with him at family gatherings, all of it good-natured. Neither of us would budge in our support for our party's candidates. My household was Democratic, his Republican. We sparred. It was fun, and I enjoyed the attention and specific kind of relationship and rapport I had with my older cousin, having no older brothers of my own.

---

4   "His views attracted the attention of wealthy Orange County conservatives such as fast-food magnate Carl Karcher, sporting goods heir Willard Voit and San Juan Capistrano rancher Tom Rogers." From "John G. Schmitz," Wikipedia, accessed February 15, 2025, https://en.wikipedia.org/wiki/John_G._Schmitz.

Bobby had been approaching a marriageable age when he died. He'd stood in the wedding of another cousin, Tim LeVecke, just two months before the accident. So many cousins, so many weddings. The event of Bill's wedding to Margaret was, as I mentioned, a Big Deal. Though they were still in active mourning, our parents had no choice but to attend. They got dressed up and put smiles on their faces, and so did I and some of my brothers and sisters. We loved our oldest cousin, Bill, even if he was a Republican. Many other Sweeney cousins were present at the reception on the large patio of the Karchers' hacienda-style home in old Anaheim.

I had a reputation in the family at large for being outspoken about my politics. It was, after all, the spring of 1970. The war in Vietnam was raging, Nixon was president, Kissinger was bombing Cambodia, and five students had just that week been shot dead at Kent State. My goals for this wedding were to keep Mom company and to avoid Carl Karcher. We knew John Schmitz would probably be there, and I had no plan to interact with him at all. I loathed both men and their stinking selfish, racist, war-mongering politics.

My cousin Donnie Fergus had other ideas. He somehow orchestrated a conversation between me and those two men, with Mom standing nearby. Donnie didn't care a bit about the politics; he was just after creating a scene. I recall that we got into a little jousting talk about the injustice of the war. Both men were sharing predictable points of view, telling me I didn't know what I was talking about. And then Mom spoke up.

"You men," she said, "need to listen to people like Patsy and the young people who do know what they're talking about. Even if you don't like the way some of them look, they're right. This war is wrong."

I have an image of my fifty-three-year-old mother with her gloved hands crossed, her purse in one and the other pointing and gesturing as she scolded Karcher and Schmitz like they were bad boys. Wow, I hadn't seen that coming.

After so much resistance and acrimony on both our parts, she'd stood up for me. I'd witnessed and empathized with her suffering over the loss of Bobby. That she demonstrated understanding and support for the antiwar movement, including for me, in that setting, with those men, astonished me. It didn't surprise me that she was against the war, but that she spoke up for me to them.

Evie, me, and Michael at Pismo Preserve, Pismo Beach, CA. November 4, 2021.

Magic Dress

1987 had been a miserable year. I was drinking too much and using too much. I was having blackouts and finding myself in questionable and even dangerous situations, in the kinds of places where I wasn't raised to be. My parents probably saw I was in trouble, but not how much. I don't think they knew about the drugs or the extent to which I'd lost control of my drinking. Mom understood it had killed me to lose my job at the alternative high school where I'd been denied tenure. I was humiliated, stunned. In spite of my drinking, which I thought I'd hid well, I'd had excellent evaluations and good rapport with students. I'd initiated creative and relevant curriculum. I got the cruel notice of my "non-reelection"[5] on March 15. I was expected to show up for work until the end of the semester, which I took as an excuse to drink more. At the conclusion of the school year and my job, I turned forty.

My mother had sent me a gift.

"I can't wait until you see it. I think you'll really like it," she'd said. "There's a new shop down here, and I got you something."

Mom's gifts were often way off the mark. Wrong size or color or style; usually too straight-looking or plain. Or maybe some odd piece of pottery she found at a shop in Morro Bay. As a child I always got the wrong bike or doll. Even the gun she bought me was wrong: I'd wanted a revolver; she got me a derringer. It was a family joke that Mother couldn't please me, that I was difficult, too fussy. An early malcontent.

I was awash in self-pity on my fortieth birthday. I went out for drinks with a fellow teacher. I ran into a male friend at the bar and spent the evening with him.

The gift from my mother waited, unopened.

---

5   Under Ed Code 44929.21, probationary employees can be non-reelected as long as they're notified by March 15, even if they have excellent reviews, are loved by students and parents, are respected by colleagues, and have never had a complaint.

"Are you having cake, dear?" she asked the next day when I called.

"Later today, Mom," I lied. "I'm going to open your gift right now."

She couldn't see how hungover I was on that late Saturday morning. Couldn't smell the sadness seeping from my pores. It was June. I had a week left of work. I opened the package, saw something purple underneath the tissue paper, and lifted out a delicate long purple dress.

"Mom, it's beautiful!" I cried. "What a pretty dress."

"We have a new shop down here, the Sea Traders, and I saw that and knew it was for you, dear daughter."

I shook out the light gauzy garment with my free hand. It was covered in symbols: hands, fish, platypus, hearts. The symbols stood out in red and blue on a dark purple background. The dress was sleeveless, had straps at the top, a flowing skirt.

"It has pockets!" I yelped. "It's really beautiful. It's so beautiful," I repeated.

"Enjoy it, Patsy dear. I hope it makes you happy. You deserve to be so happy."

"I can't wait to wear it. Thank you so much." I found myself holding back tears.

At the time I had a diabetic trash-devouring dog, a roommate who drank more than I did, and a car worth seventy-five dollars that was covered with someone else's bumper stickers: "Goonie," "Take A Chill Pill," "Totally Rad, Psyche!," "I am the Evil Twin," "Awesome!," a partial inventory. The car was an old Maverick, once red, its hood secured with a fat, greasy rope. The hood whapped up and down when it picked up speed.

I'd made it through the school year by falling down the stairs and getting a hematoma on my butt, which had resulted in my drinking brandy in bed and using up all my sick leave. At graduation, the principal of the small alternative school presented me with an engraved mug: "To Ms. T, with Affection and Appreciation." Pictures of that event show a woman with a forced smile, a red bloated face, and smooth blonde hair. The simple truth is I drank and used for twenty years, at first with relief and exhilaration. By the end, it was a compulsion.

But all was not lost—not yet. My job at the school might've come to a demoralizing end, but I'd secured a summer job coordinating vocational and career activities for students posted to various organizations and businesses around the county. I'd worked for the same agency the previous summer, and it sounded like this assignment would be a breeze. I was in a wine-tasting group with the person who hired me.

Prior to starting work with the kids, we staff were expected to bond by participating in a team-building ropes course exercise. The very notion of a ropes course was anathema to me. It wasn't my style to perform "trust" by falling backward off a tree stump into the arms of well-meaning colleagues; or, worse yet, by climbing one hundred feet up a tree to zip through the woods on suspended wires. I did not get excited or feel accomplished when log-walking or standing on an aluminum disc nailed into a three-foot stump without losing my balance. The ropes course was, however, a means to an end. I figured I'd endure it like I had so many days in the past year, by just getting through.

On the morning of the ropes course, I couldn't get out of bed. I was drunk from the night before, sick, hungover. It was more than that, though. I was wholly exhausted by life. Done in. I called in sick. Turns out calling in sick for a required team-building activity is crossing a line. The two supervisors running the summer program summoned me to a meeting. Long story short, they liked me but thought I needed help. They cut me loose.

Now I'd really been fired for the first time in my life. Fired. Me. I could justify the non-reelect notice from the school district as a bureaucratic maneuver to have fewer tenured teachers on payroll. It didn't make me happy, but there was a way of looking at it that wasn't personal. Fired, though! This time I'd truly screwed up.

I was mortified. I knew I needed to stop drinking, at least for a while. To give it a rest. What would life be without good wine?

The supervisor who'd hired me for the summer position, my wine-tasting cohort, offered to help me find a place for treatment. I went voluntarily, though I didn't have a lot of options. I had no money and nowhere else to go. I wasn't eager to return to my parents' house at age forty. We spent part of a day driving around the county and visiting the few local treatment options, stopping for drinks along the way. Once I made my choice, she and my sister Evie, who'd agreed to take charge of my dog Lulu, dropped me off at rehab.

It was a hot drive—from Healdsburg through Alexander Valley, across a major artery of wine country, a sharp left at Calistoga, up the Silverado Trail to St. Helena, and left again up Deer Park Road, at the top of which sat my destination for that summer, St. Helena Recovery Center. I'd had a few beers that afternoon so wasn't completely sober when I arrived. I wore the deep purple sundress, the gift from my mother. I was tired, red-faced, defeated, and a bit high. I had no agenda besides knowing I needed a break from what had become an inexplicable two bottles of Sauvignon Blanc (or anything else available) a night. I figured I just needed to push the pause button; I'd be back to nice wine by Thanksgiving.

I swiveled in a chair nervously as one of the clinical staff checked me in, the dress billowing around me. Then, suddenly, the enormity of what I was doing overtook my restlessness. My sandaled feet went still on the floor. Something I couldn't name swept up and away from me. I heard and felt a whoosh as it rushed up and out, passing through my legs, belly, chest, neck, and head, into the lights and ceiling, and on out to the summer night's sky. I shivered and sank back into my seat, patted my red puffy cheeks, and let my hands fall to my lap and rest on one of the dress's symbols. My entire being calmed and sighed. I couldn't begin to divine its message at that time, but some higher order was signaling to me.

I wore the purple dress again when Mom and Daddy came to

visit on one of the facility's Family Sundays. I continued to choose it for summer occasions for as long as it fit me. Evie dubbed it "the magic dress." I loaned it to her with great caution and infrequency, and only for special celebrations that didn't include me. I would not let her wash it. The magic dress rests on a shelf in my closet as I write this, evocative of the suntan lotion of earlier years, a powerful totem of my sobriety and Mom's intuitive genius.

God willing, I had my final drink (and nonprescription drug) on July 7, 1987.

Maureen: Big Sister

In many of our childhood photographs, while a pretty Maureen smiles at the camera, I appear disgruntled, scowling. In at least one, I have a dirty face. Maureen's unyielding goodness made room for me to be reactive, rebellious and, I'll admit, resentful. She got everything first and best from dolls to bikes to compliments.

Everyone just loved Maureen. She was the "good girl." The first of the eight of us, she was one of the first grandchildren and thus doted on by parents, grandmothers, aunties, and uncles. We were eighteen months apart, and our parents dressed us alike. I also wore her hand-me-downs. We took sewing, tennis, and piano classes together. We were invited on outings with unmarried aunts and Nana Truxaw. We sat, two skinny blondes, fifteen and sixteen years old, in the back seat of Nana's Buick for a trip to the 1962 Seattle World's Fair.

We were in tandem all through school, Maureen always two years ahead of me, including at the only girls' Catholic high school in Anaheim, Marywood. Maureen played the piano with passion, enduring the not-always-affectionate mockery of some siblings when she practiced early and intensely in the morning or too late in the evening or at some other wrong time. We occasionally played duets at recitals. She became such an accomplished pianist that she received a four-year scholarship to the University of Portland.

I got involved in debates, the student newspaper, and leadership. I learned to love politics and JFK and the Beatles. Maureen shared none of those interests when she was young.

Mom liked Maureen's friends and thought mine were, with few exceptions, weird.

"Why don't you have normal friends like your sister? That girl is just strange."

I liked that one was funny and off-kilter and another smart and sassy.

"I don't know so-and-so's parents." They were not Catholic and were from out of state.

I was happy when Maureen left for college in the fall of 1963. After sixteen years, I no longer had to share a room. (Maureen and I slept in half of the large girls' bedroom, which at a certain point had been separated down the middle by a temporary wall, two girls on each side.) Finally, a little space to myself, except when Maureen came home on break. When she did, she'd toss her stuff on the bed and say, "Well, Patricia, what's going on? Which of my clothes did you take while I was gone?"

"Just a few things," I'd confess. I was always surprisingly happy to see her. It was a comfort to have her around for a week or two. My feelings toward Maureen were mixed from an early age.

When it was my turn to go to college, I didn't get away. I headed to the new UC campus at Irvine and lived at Janss Way for the first year. The summer before I started, Maureen surprised me with a gift of a nubby sweater from Joseph Magnin, a stylish pullover I wore for years beyond its wearable lifespan. Even though we were close in age, she was more a creature of the fifties and I the sixties. When Mom would be angry or "disappointed" in me, Maureen wouldn't take sides, but she'd attempt to coach me to moderate my conduct. In those college days, Maureen was kind and smooth, mature. She

Maureen playing piano at Janss Way. 1970. Visit my website www.forgivemess.com to hear an audio clip of Maureen at the piano.

had a knack for getting along while being bossy. When I was hanging out with longhairs whom my mother regarded as a bad influence, Mom sent me with Bobby on that train to Portland to spend spring break under Maureen's guidance.

"Why can't you be more like Maureen?" I heard a time too many.

Maureen was living in an apartment in Anaheim when Bobby was killed. But she was at Janss Way when the call came about the accident and stayed while Mom, Daddy, and Johnny went to the hospital. By then she'd graduated from Portland and was a new elementary schoolteacher. Sometime during the wake-like gathering of extended family at the house the next morning, Uncle Noel (my godfather and Mom's younger brother) pulled Maureen aside for a lecture.

"Now, you need to take care of your mother. She's going to need a lot of support and help. You're the oldest," he said. "It falls to you."

Maureen looking good at Devils Postpile National Monument in Mammoth Lakes, CA. Probably late 1960s.

I have just a few distinct images from that day, and none of them include Maureen. The sole image I have of Uncle Noel is of him refreshing his drink. If he'd said anything like that to me, I would've sloughed it off, just as I had when Mom sent him down to Irvine to persuade me to stop hanging around students she'd decided were a bad influence. At the time I'd felt like I was being stalked, and I knew he was wrong. But his message to me wasn't so different from the one he laid on Maureen: "You must do this for your mother."

I don't recall hearing about or understanding the significant impact of Uncle Noel's words on Maureen until we were older. It was years later, when she was distraught, that she'd dredge up the memory. She'd evoke his directive bitterly, woefully, a message that still echoed in her mind as a burden she'd been forced to carry. One curse of the first daughter in our family was compliance.

"But why would you think Uncle Noel was right? He doesn't know what he's talking about," I'd say, trying to be helpful.

"It really messed me up, Patsy," she'd whimper. "You just don't understand what it did to me."

~~~~~~~

After Bobby's funeral, I stayed around Janss Way for a day or so and then headed back to Newport and school. I came by the house more often than usual, but I wasn't there day in and day out as the family adjusted, or didn't adjust, to Bobby's sudden absence. I was adjusting, too, but pretty much on my own. Maureen was around Janss Way at a time when our parents weren't fully functioning, which I would learn she resented.

The overarching theme of this family memoir is how deeply and differently the loss of Bobby affected each of us. It was devastating to Maureen. Like the rest of us, her life was disrupted. She was a first-year teacher, starting out on her own after going to college out of state for four years. Suddenly, Bobby's death drew her back to her parents and siblings. She married in 1971 and continued teaching elementary school. Her life journey includes marriage, two children, work, multiple moves, divorce, physical and mental distress, and a slow road to addiction.

Maureen felt ferociously betrayed and angry when she discovered her husband had been having an affair with a coworker. Mom shared her worries about Maureen with me over the years, especially once I got sober in 1987 and was no longer a family worry myself. She called one night to tell me Maureen had intentionally overdosed on Tylenol. Mom pleaded with me to go see her. I drove the three hundred-plus miles from Healdsburg to Santa Maria the next day, arriving at Maureen's in the afternoon. She was tired and teary and said she'd like her life to be more like mine.

In the parlance of recovery, she wanted what I had. That night, with her consent, I took Maureen to an Alcoholics Anonymous meeting. She'd been drinking more than usual, had conflict at her teaching job, was angry and resentful toward her ex-husband, and was making life difficult for her kids, Annie and Bobby. They'd come home from tennis lessons the day before to find an ambulance at their house. She'd never been a heavy drinker like I was, but she was anxious, aggrieved, and miserable. Was she really an alcoholic? That wasn't for me to say. I didn't have anything else to offer; AA was working for me, and I knew many members' primary drug of choice wasn't booze.

She liked AA meetings right away and got a sponsor. She listened, she lightened up, and her life got on an even keel. It was an amazing transformation. Maureen and her kids thrived. Annie graduated and moved on to UC Santa Barbara, and Bobby finished high school. Maureen and her ex, Bobby's father, attended his graduation, and we were all relieved to see the decorum Maureen exercised during the postgraduation celebration.

We threw Maureen a surprise party when she turned fifty in 1996. She'd come a long way, and the party was both recognition and celebration. Maureen loved swimming in the ocean, so Mom suggested we pitch in and get her a wetsuit. We chose a black one with a smidgeon of purple and red trim. Her birthday is in January, but that didn't stop her from trying it out right away.

Our family's stories weave and overlap in strands of expected and unexpected episodes; commemoration and disruption exist side by side. Much of our history is pixelated with bittersweet or tainted events. On Maureen's birthday weekend, while on the train from Carlsbad to San Luis Obispo County for the party, our brother Paul received word that he'd been let go from his job of twenty-plus years. He was devastated but participated in the festivities. Maureen was the star, and her birthday party was void of major drama. At fifty, Maureen was looking good.

So, what happened? Annie was away at college, Bobby married Katie, Maureen moved from Santa Maria to Bakersfield to the Sacramento area to be nearer to Annie. She quit going to meetings. She had a pain in her head. She went to specialists. She had surgeries. She became addicted to pain medication. She was in a state of emotional whiplash, at times loving, cruel, nasty, apologetic. Embarrassing. Exhausting. I've edited out details from an earlier version of this book of her eruptions at family dinners, her blaming and screaming, and the emotional upheaval and abuse for those who tolerated, loved, and tried to help her. I've lost track of the number of times I helped her move, or moved her, or visited or transported her with Annie to another rehab. She "fell asleep" at the table during a holiday meal with Bobby, Katie, and their young child, Jacob. She stopped coming to family gatherings, claiming she had "the flu."

Maureen made attempts to carry on. She went back to school and got a master's degree in special education. She and Annie traveled to Mexico to snorkel. We took a sisters' trip to Cabo San Lucas to celebrate Maureen's sixty-fifth birthday and Evie's cancer remission. (You'll read about Evie in a later chapter.)

For years she cooked a traditional beef Wellington–like meal for Mom's birthday. We'd walk on the beach and talk and talk and laugh. She wanted to be my friend. She didn't host holiday meals, but she always brought a hostess gift when she came to our house. She was almost always my fan. She and her kids sent me cards when I was in rehab in 1987. She sent more birthday cards to family members than any of us. She encouraged me to be grateful for John, my husband, when I complained. For years, the earth-toned pottery bowl we used for salads was one she gave me for my fiftieth birthday. She played "Climb Every Mountain" on the family piano with authority and joy.

Maureen had ailments and went to doctors the way others have hobbies. She never bought street drugs. She became addicted to pain medications prescribed by multiple medical doctors she saw for her variety of symptoms. Her head, her surgeries, her stomach, her low oxygen levels, her neck. Norco. Flu, diarrhea, acupuncture, rehabs, lashing out, apologizing, blaming. Norco. We had her try THC and Suboxone—she said they didn't help. I suggested she go to meetings again, get a dog. I'd drive one hundred miles to visit her in Sacramento, and once we swam in the pool where she was living. She was in the habit of calling on Annie to take her to the ER.

Annie hired a nurse to go to Maureen's house and administer her medications on a regular schedule. The medication was locked in a safe. I'm not sure why this didn't work, but it didn't. Maureen spent time in three rehabs and was asked to leave at least one. After the final rehab attempt failed, Annie and Bobby were almost done trying. As a stipulation for staying in their lives, Maureen moved into an assisted living facility with medication management. Her histrionic opposition and complaints began the first morning there (I witnessed them), and later staff found forbidden drugs during a search. Maureen wasn't compliant. Her oppositional behaviors persisted. She left assisted living for a senior apartment in Sacramento.

Maureen showed up to spend time with Mom the last week of Mom's life in 2014. She also made it to Mom's memorial, dragging an oxygen tank, but didn't participate in its planning or production, or in the closing of our parents' home and the disposition of its contents. She told me what she wanted over the phone, and I packed it for her. She did arrange for the piano to be moved to her house in Sacramento. Even through some of her worst days and times, I saw glimpses of the Maureen I knew as a cohort in the family, as the older sister who could look me in the eye and reach my heart, but our roles in the family had undergone a reversal. No one ever abandoned her.

We rented a large oceanfront house at Newport for a gathering of our whole tribe the week between Christmas and New Year's in 2015, the year after Mom died. Maureen had been excited about coming. The day before we all convened, she sent an email with her regrets citing "incredible pain" from failing discs. She said she'd miss walking on the beach with me and asked that I send pictures. She promised to pay a deposit to rent the house for the following year. Everyone was there but her, including spouses and baby Logan and young Jacob.

Disappointment and sadness are inadequate descriptions for how I felt. She missed a good one.

She was found dead by Annie in November 2017. She was seventy-one years old.

The last call I had from her, she wanted to know if she should see a naturopath. I was shopping for groceries.

"If you think it would help," was all I had to offer. "Take care, Maureen," I said. "Let's talk later, okay?"

"But what do you think?" she insisted.

"If you think it will help," I repeated without much conviction. "Take care."

As if she hadn't heard what I really thought she should do a million times before. Go outside. Go to a meeting. Take a walk. Volunteer. Find a purpose. I no longer thought she should get a dog.

Maureen remembered to wish our brother Michael a happy birthday on November 4, 2017. That weekend she left Annie phone and text messages saying she felt strange and needed help. Annie had rescued her so many times. Maureen didn't pick up Annie's return calls. Maybe she was angry and ignoring them. Annie phoned several more times, and then on November 7 she drove over to her mother's house, where she found what she'd dreaded.

The turnout for Maureen's memorial surprised me in a good

way, considering how she'd been exhausting some of us for years. Cousins who were contemporaries on both sides of the family showed up at Holy Sepulcher Cemetery, where Johnny had gotten a plot for Maureen's ashes in the same gravesite as our brother Bobby's, near our parents and other Truxaws and Sweeneys. More people showed up after the funeral at Bobby and Katie's house not too far away. It was comforting to hear their stories of escapades with Maureen, and their fondness and respect for her. Our cousins had no idea what the end of her life had been like, and their laughter and memories were untinged with disillusion, regret, and relief. Maybe that's when my perception of my sister started becoming whole again.

A few weeks after Maureen's memorial, I'm rinsing out a marine-blue vase. Its bulb shape fits solidly and securely in both palms. I work a bottle brush gently through its narrow neck into the base. Milky white interior, and the loveliest turquoise hues outside. Warm soapy water. I hear Maureen's voice: "Hey, Patricia." Her teasing is rich with affection, and a tug of grief rises from my heart to my throat. She gave me the vase years ago at one of the holiday dinners John and I hosted.

I'm no longer angry at my sister for not getting it together. Why was I able to get and stay sober and she wasn't? I miss her and wish things had turned out differently. What if she'd been diagnosed as bipolar? What if that had been it? And the question I always ask: What if our family had been exposed to grief counseling? The wiring in our family is fragile; it's an inheritance I've had to adjust to. We have a predisposition to mental illness and addiction. From what I now understand about Norco, a trade name for hydrocodone, is that although it's weaker than oxycontin, it's still a highly addictive opioid. This was Maureen's drug of choice.

When I saw Annie and Bobby at a family reunion a few years ago, they brought me Maureen's wet suit. I was grateful to have it and said I hoped to get into the water like their mom did.

"Remember the time Mom was out in the water at Morro Bay?" Annie asked. "She was waving, so everyone on shore waved back. Mom kept waving and waving, and when she finally came in she said, 'Why didn't anyone rescue me? I was in a riptide and waving for help.'"

I've yet to try out Maureen's wet suit. I'm now by default the big sister.

Paul: Significant Brother

Before I understood later in life that Paul was a kind guy, as well as a goofy guy, I didn't believe we had a lot in common. He's the second of my four brothers, born a year and three weeks after Bobby. Paul hated school right from the start. Some mornings he'd run naked, circling through the living room, into the kitchen, rounding the built-in Formica table where most of us were having breakfast, on into the family room, and back again to the living room. His small naked body would dash around as he chanted, "Peepee-doodie meatloaf, peepee doodie meatloaf," or some other nonsensical incantation, his eyes bright with defiance and challenge.

"Paul," Mom would say, "go put some clothes on. You're going to school."

As I've mentioned, Paul often ate dinner at the breadboard across from the Formica table and had specially prepared meals. He didn't want foods to touch, refused to eat meatloaf. In retrospect, he was a nervous little boy, which may explain why he developed asthma. He also uttered provocative words when fully clothed, ones he thankfully didn't use as he got older. Paul was one of the blonds and cute before maturing into good-looking. He was the least liberal and most straight. He became the most "normal" of us seven remaining siblings.

I considered myself superior to Paul because I liked school and did well, whereas he struggled. He was a relentless tease at home, taunting Maureen as she practiced the piano, or calling Evie "Hazelnut," which would get a rise out of her every time. I desperately didn't want him to make fun of me and managed to evade much of his verbal jabbing, until he latched on to deriding me about a college friend who was quirky and overweight. This behavior vanished, I think, because of maturity and lack of an audience.

Although he wasn't an ace student academically, Paul was chatty and affable, had a great smile, and was a social success—still is. He was good pals with our cousins Jim Fergus and Eddie Mari, and with Bobby too. A gang of boys played football in the backyard and baseball in the cul-de-sac in front of our house for years. The Turkey Bowl, a touch football game on Thanksgiving morning at the high school near Janss Way, became a neighborhood and family tradition. Most of the Sweeney cousins lived within walking distance. It seemed like my brothers were always outside playing or mowing the lawn. Paul was a cutup, a joker, the one who'd stick a finger in his nose during a family picture. This is a habit he's refined with time, technology, and maturity. His primary focus of teasing these days is himself.

When I was a student at Irvine in 1967 and living at the family beach house in Newport, Paul was a senior at Servite High School. He convinced me I would be very cool if I let him and his friends have an after-prom party at the oceanfront. Two of our cousins attended the girls' school and were dates of Servite boys—the schools shared a common prom. It was a wildly memorable party, only in part because it resulted in a large hole in a wall beyond the ability of the partygoers to repair without notifying some of the landlords, which included all of Daddy's siblings and, of course, our parents. I and my poor judgment were blamed for the debacle, even though Paul and I had conspired in the event. For the record, I did not attend the party and was horrified to return late that night to find girls in fancy dresses wobbling around, including a disheveled one exiting a bedroom.

Another time, when Paul and I were home alone for a week working summer jobs, the others off on a family vacation, a loud banging on the front door jarred me from sleep. When I ran to investigate, Paul stumbled in and vomited all over the entryway. *What a dope,* I thought as I got him and the mess cleaned up. That could've been a bonding incident, and I did keep quiet about it, but I don't recall any significant improvement to our sibling connection.

Then Bobby died. It was Paul who picked me up at the Orange County Airport after I flew home from a work trip in San Francisco. Paul had been out that Friday night at a drive-in movie with Peggy, his future wife. They "didn't see much of the movie," he told me recently, and he doesn't remember what the picture was. He got the news about Bobby when he arrived home at one in the morning and lights were still on. Our attempts to talk while sharing the front seat of his Chevy together as we drove back to Janss Way from the airport probably sharpened the reality of Bobby's death for both of us, but I have no memory of the specifics of our conversation. We were both numb and inexperienced with personal tragedy.

Paul, our silly brother, at age nineteen, was suddenly the oldest boy.

I was finishing an extra year at UC Irvine at the time, completing a few credits and moving from managing to full editor of the *New University* newspaper. Paul was interested in speech and radio, and even though neither of them were Irvine students, he landed a show for himself and our cousin Jim at the student radio station on the same floor as the newspaper office. It was a short-lived and offbeat effort that showcased his initiative, humor, and bravado.

A few years later, in 1973, I was back in California after three years in Washington, DC, and taking a teaching credential program. Paul, who by then was married and had a job selling freight, reached out to suggest we get together for happy hour. It was an awkward meeting, something we never would have done if Bobby were still alive. While it was a good impulse on his part to attempt a connection, we weren't quite ready. Neither of us had the words, knowledge, or tools yet for sharing our grief, if that's what that meeting was meant to accomplish. By the time we parted, we were both somewhat blitzed.

Paul and Michael ready for tennis in Morro Bay, CA. Early 1980s.

By Christmas 1981, the whole family except for Paul had abandoned Anaheim and Southern California. Paul and Peggy hosted the family holiday gathering at their house in Fullerton with their two young children, Brian and David. (Erin would be born in 1983.) I was sharing a house in San Francisco with Amanda at the time; we were among a small group buying a co-op in Noe Valley. Amanda is the friend Mom thought was a bad influence. While Mom wasn't right about everything, Amanda did introduce me to cocaine a few years prior.

"Hey, P. T.," she'd said excitedly. "You've got to try this."

I remember exactly where I was sitting, at the dining table in the pretty little house in the Oakland Hills where I lived with my then-husband Mark, looking out the window. Cocaine soon became an accompaniment to many activities, and Christmas 1981 at Paul's was no exception.

Amanda and I flew down to Orange County for the day. We did a line or two before heading to the airport. Amanda dropped me off at Paul's before driving on to Anaheim in a rental car to visit her mother. She'd be back later to pick me up for our return flight. In and out, I thought as I entered Paul and Peggy's with a few packages in tow. In and out, short and sweet. Maybe a quick snort in the bathroom. I was wearing summer clothes in December to honor the Orange County sun, a brightly colored shirt and turquoise rayon pants.

"What'd you bring me, a subscription to some lefty magazine you haven't paid for?" Paul asked, eying me warily.

True, I'd given him an unpaid subscription to the progressive *Ramparts* magazine many years earlier.

"No," I said. "I got the kids some books, and you a bong."

"Why didn't Amanda come in? Is she too good for us?"

He appeared to be drinking coffee, possibly laced with brandy following Daddy's practice. Though not a big drinker, Daddy would always fix a holiday cocktail on Christmas morning.

"Would you like some hot chocolate?" Peggy stepped in. "It's the holiday special. Don't you look like a summer girl, Patsy, and so thin!"

"It's an unusually warm December, isn't it?" I said, passing on the hot chocolate. It looked like everyone in the family was there. The children were sweet and adorable. The youngest one, David, was a ringer for Paul's baby pictures. I hadn't seen much of their kids at all—I'd been busy getting divorced, moving, holding down a program specialist job, and more. Everything in their house was perfect, color-coordinated, and decorated in blues, greens, and beiges. There were family pictures galore. I noticed a mini shrine to Bobby set up on a table as I flitted around the edges, which wasn't hard to do. In a family as large as ours, a person can feel invisible.

I complimented Peggy on the house, sat and watched the boys open gifts. I waited for time to pass so I could leave. Mom observed how nice I looked and asked about life in the city. Daddy offered me a drink and gave me a look. He saw me. At a certain point when all of us "kids" were outside taking a group picture, suddenly we all mooned an invisible antagonist. Johnny, Paul, Evie, me, pants down, butts bared, ridiculous. There's a picture to prove it. Maureen and Michael stand at opposite ends of our line, fully clothed and smiling.

I heard the toot of a horn. Amanda was outside.

Maybe I'd been too giddy, too bright. As I said goodbyes and made to leave, Paul took me aside at the door and said, "Peg and I don't want you around our children when you're like this. You're a mess and a bad example."

Then I was out the door. My heart pounded in shame.

"Let's get out of here. I need a drink," I told Amanda.

My brother and I didn't speak for several years.

As happens in life and in families, Time Passed.

I got sober.

At some point I made perfunctory amends to Paul. I couldn't tell if he forgave me.

We were cordial but not close when we saw each other at family gatherings.

Paul was laid off in 1996 from a sales job he'd had for more than twenty years. As I mentioned, he got the news while on the train to Maureen's fiftieth birthday party. He'd been hurt, felt betrayed, and was worried about supporting his family. That he didn't let this life-disrupting news dampen Maureen's special weekend caught my attention and prompted me to see him in a different light. He'd still make unenlightened and sarcastic digs about our gay brothers, Michael and Johnny, though.

The family was set to gather again for Johnny's fiftieth birthday party in late April 2003 at the house in the Oakland Hills he shared with David, his partner and future husband. I heard from Mom that Paul was still struggling financially and might not make the party. Sales work had dried up, so he was working as a custodian at a local school and at night security jobs. I had unused air miles, so on a whim I called Paul and volunteered them for his travel to the party. It was easily arranged. I also offered him a bed in Healdsburg, where I lived with my partner and future husband John.

It was a test of sorts. I had the resources, and he had the need, and surprisingly he agreed. Maybe I had something to prove; if so, I wasn't totally certain what it was. Maybe I was simply being kind. He must have reached some kind of inner truce regarding Johnny's sexuality by then; otherwise, he would've stayed home. Unlike Michael, who'd only ever had male partners, Johnny was once married to a woman. He came out after he and his wife split up. Paul had a difficult time accepting this, but he ultimately agreed with Mom when she said, "He's your brother. Get over it. I'm not wild about it either." I know Paul invited Johnny to one of his kid's graduations.

When I drove Paul back to Oakland for his flight out the morning after the party, he thanked me and said it had been good seeing me. A few months later one of his boys dropped by for the night on a tour of skate parks.

~~~~~~~~~~

Driving toward the ocean on a radiant Sunday morning in August 2006, I noted Paul's redness, his proximity, his babble. He seemed almost comical, endearing. We were headed to a deli. He gave me directions while manically scratching his hands and arms, rubbing them nervously, chattering away. It was just the two of us. I'd driven down to Carlsbad the day prior, chauffeuring Mom and Marguerite to the annual Sweeney Family Picnic that would be held later that morning.

When she was still alive, I periodically stepped up to drive Mom to family gatherings and funerals in and around Anaheim and the neighborhoods Mom and Daddy had abandoned for the Central Coast back in the '70s. Mom still had a few remaining siblings down south, plus their children and extensive progeny, most of whom no one in our immediate family could even identify. My brothers and sisters would not or could not ferry Mom around like this—they only rarely made the effort to attend this event. In those days, Mom and Marguerite were a package deal. They lived and traveled together.

I'd missed years of these gatherings myself, riddled as they were with a surfeit of Catholic cousins and aunts, most of whom boycotted my first marriage to a non-Catholic. There were so many Republicans and children; so many straight, successful people who still went to church, admired both George Bushes, Ronald Reagan, even Nixon. Over time and with the emotional maturity that can accompany sobriety, my fondness for the cousins, aunties, and uncles I'd grown up with began to override my distaste for their retro politics. And besides, it turned out a few were actually

Democrats. The tug-of-war in my heart and brain pulled strongly toward family in later life, but I still had some judgy issues to work on. It's a lifelong project.

But this is about Paul. Paul was the holdout, the sole remnant of our immediate family who still lived down south. Even he eventually left Orange County, but where we others had gone north, Paul went as far south as he could get without crossing over into Mexico.

Our family had been tasked to buy provisions—sandwich makings and drinks—from a place my niece recommended. Each family brings their own meal to the Sweeney Family Picnic, plus something extra to share. I figured our something to share was our ninety-year-old mother.

I was surprised and pleased when Paul volunteered to run the errand with me. He continued to scratch his hands and arms, which were badly inflamed. Cocooned in the comfort of my car, he unleashed a torrent of conversation. Was my car new? What about those Padres? Have I been to any Giants games? Why'd I get rid of the Subaru? Remember his Beretta? The kids refused to drive or ride in it. He'd been desperate when he bought that car so cheap. How'd I like my new car? I only half-listened to my brother's jabber. Had he become a compulsive talker? It looked like he'd put on weight.

It was a stunningly beautiful Southern California Sunday morning. A slight sea damp misted the air. An energizing chill beneath an early sun, a faint smell of salt. I didn't want to be reflective, but a memory washed through me. *That* memory. I'm walking away from Paul's house in Fullerton. He doesn't want me around his children. Neither does Peggy. They think I'm a bad influence on their kids. It stung because it was true. *That* memory is a big one on the inventory of behaviors that keeps me sober. I'd resented Paul for saying that. Hated him. I still had mixed feelings about him.

Consciously or not, the past is always there, the whole history, in every moment, a collection of dark and light, misstep and progress, regret and resolution. But I was long sober and sorry.

I continued to make amends in part by showing up. I mostly felt calm, good about myself and my place in the family. And what a gorgeous morning. I was grateful to be with my brother.

"Maybe they'll have something for my skin here," he said, directing me to pull into a health food store and deli. "What do you think I should get? The doctor says it's psoriasis. Whatever it is, it just won't go away. It's all over my legs, back, everywhere, and the itching is driving me crazy. I took one of Peg's tranquilizers. Anyway, you know about healthy things, so what do you think?"

"Arnica," I suggested. "Or Calendula. That's supposed to be soothing."

"There's something else I need to talk to you about, Patsy, but you can't tell anyone, OK? No one knows."

He'd never confided in me. Ever. We'd rarely had a serious conversation. *Maybe one of the kids is gay. That would serve him right,* my wicked side thought.

"OK, Paul," I said. "Might as well lay it on me. What do you got?"

We stayed put in the car.

He took a deep breath, rubbed and scratched at his arms some more.

I noticed again that it looked like he'd gained weight. We were so near the coast I could smell the salt air. I put the windows down, letting the morning sea breeze in.

Then my brother proceeded to share concerns he and Peggy had about one of their children, something he didn't feel comfortable talking about with anyone else, he said. I offered him some advice and recommendations, as I would do, and have often done, for parents of former students and friends with children. I honored what a big deal it was for him to say, "Well, here goes," and unburden himself to me.

Paul expressed some anguish and confusion about the situation. It became clear to me that he worried about his children all the time. His anxiety was almost palpable. I realized this was something we shared: We're both nervous worriers. He has the bad family wiring too. We had a real conversation there in the car.

If I tell you I was strangely elated, how weird is that?

"Paul," I said, unlocking the door. "After we take care of your skin and get the food, we can keep talking."

"And I need to tell you," he said quickly. "I never should've spoken to you the way I did that Christmas. I should've offered to help you."

"No, you did the right thing. It got me to look at myself," I said, and it was true. "At the time it felt awful, but you were doing what you needed to do to protect your kids. Your words stung, but they rang in my head and helped me get sober. It's important to tell the truth."

~~~~~~~

Paul and I spent hours together during Mom's decline when we were both visiting and helping. We bought the Christmas tree together. We walked all over Morro Bay, from motel rooms to dinner and back. We sorted boxes from the garage together, helped plan the memorial, consoled each other. We were both listening to Van Morrison's "Celtic New Year." He insulated me from another brother's hurtful jabs. I respect Paul's fierce loyalty to his family— to Peggy, to their three kids, and now to three beloved grandkids who all benefit from his humor, humanity, and heart. He's a significant brother and, as it turns out, a Democrat.

Paul and Peggy's home, in particular their patio and pool in Carlsbad, is a happy destination for celebrations and a fixture in the lives of their kids and three grandchildren. Paul's silliness and sense of play, including sports, spreads like happy contagion. His daughter Erin, a special education teacher and now a mother, initiated a fantasy football league called All in the Family. It includes three generations of family, is ridiculous competitive fun, and provides intense comic relief. Once reluctant family members have joined too. Erin, the commissioner (or Commish, as Evie calls her) keeps it real and silly. Yes, she is her father's daughter. I hear Paul mows her lawn.

Paul reluctantly wearing a Dodgers cap in Morro Bay, CA.
October 2024.

Evie: Mission

"Didn't you used to live around here?" Evie asks.

I glance up at the street sign, but nothing looks familiar. She's telling me about the taqueria Papalote she chose for lunch, and I'm only half listening. I'm thinking about the difference between loss and grief. Loss can be gotten over, but grief is like a seed with permanent roots. It's stored in memory and in our hearts, in the physical body. Grief is the rich deposit left even when loss is recovered or survived.

"It won the Food Network's burrito throwdown," she says.

Evie is a foodie married to an organic farmer whose specialty is chiles.[6] She runs the family farm stand. At today's appointment, Dr. Powell told her to lose weight. Given the last year of surgery, chemotherapy, CA-125s, CAT scans, supplemental foods, therapies, and positive thoughts, this is a good-news day. A miracle. An enormous sigh of relief. She's in remission. We're celebrating with lunch.

---

6   This vignette was written in 2012. Evie is no longer married to Farmer Wayne, but she's still a foodie and supportive of the farm in Sonoma County.

"I'm sure your place was nearby. Somewhere over there." She points west. "Here's Papalote."

We're at the corner of Twenty-Fourth and Valencia Streets in San Francisco's Mission District. We examine the small restaurant from the outside and, without speaking, agree to enter. It's crowded, and my eyes soon sting from the smoky haze of grilled chicken and peppers. Evie's are watering, too, so maybe she won't notice I'm fighting back tears.

I lived in this city thirty years ago and now have trouble getting my bearings. I'd needed Google Maps to locate Kaiser Medical Center the first time I drove Evie to the gynecologic oncology specialist even though I'd been there myself in the '80s. It was around the corner from Divisadero on Geary. In the old days I had a flawless sense of direction, intuitively homing in on dealers on either side of the Bay. It was later, after I got sober, that a sickening disturbance beset me, a haphazard neuron misfiring. An old song, or a street sign, or an innocent question might trigger a troubling memory, and I'd be lost.

"Wasn't it on Twenty-Fifth? I remember walking to the Mission from your old place," Evie presses.

"You do?"

The year of my divorce from Mark, 1980, was a reckless one for me. I moved from Oakland to Potrero Hill, and then to Noe Valley. I'd been promoted out of the classroom to supervise a program for at-risk students for which, it turned out, there was no funding. A manager later found guilty of embezzlement had redirected grant funds to himself. So, I had a job but little to do. We all dabbled with cocaine in the early '80s. Amanda brought some with her when she moved back west from Washington, DC, and soon it was a given when friends gathered—and sometimes even with family. I called in sick frequently and with impunity. I had time, money, a new habit, and no students. A perfect storm of opportunity and excuse for a budding addict, and on the list of my shameful behaviors.

Evie making Thanksgiving gravy in my Santa Rosa kitchen. November 2010.

~~~~~~

We're finally at Papalote's counter, where I order chicken tacos. Evie questions the woman taking orders about every item on the menu. My sister cannot purchase a pair of pants or a sweater or a carpet or a paint color or an appliance without going through a complex sorting process, one that might involve phone calls and emailed pictures or texts to friends and relatives. Evie is thrifty and can be downright cheap. But she's witty and self-mocking in her pitiful indecision. I'm practical, self-contained, and self-conscious. I had a prolonged adolescence and spend what I make, leaving little in reserve. She's effusive, gabby, social. She has savings.

Evie orders a bean burrito. "Go light on the cheese," she says. "I'm recovering from cancer, doctor's orders."

The waitress blanches. Evie's directness can make people uncomfortable. It's a large-family survival tactic she learned long ago. I cringe in silence. This was the year, if ever, to indulge her quirky impulses.

I'd had an intimation Evie had cancer before her diagnosis. I woke up one morning in 2007 with a headline scrolling across my inner vision. "Evie has cancer," I told my husband. "Maybe we should cancel our trip to Paris."

It wasn't the first time I'd received a message like this, and my intuition had proven prophetic in the past. Plus, I remembered how an astrologer had asked me the previous year whether someone in the family was sick, or whether I'd been ill.

"Hmm, not that I know of," I said.

"Well, someone might be sick or about to get sick," he said, flat and matter-of-factly.

Not wanting to freak Evie out in case I was having auditory hallucinations or early onset dementia (as I've mentioned, the wiring in our family is a mess), I said nothing about the warning. Just in case, I visited Evie more often, observing her with great scrutiny. Just the usual unplucked hairs, runner's legs, swimmer's arms, dirty shoes, and pencil-lipped Evie Truxaw smile. Other than the facial hairs and dirty shoes, I envied how she looked.

Then there was a lump on her breast and a biopsy. The results came while John and I were in Paris. It wasn't cancer but calcification. I bought her a small stylish shirt from one of the shops on Rue du Passy, a little fringy thing, a hint of turquoise, girly. I delivered it to the farm stand where she was selling summer crops from a rustic lean-to bathed in willows on the side of a dusty road, the toilet an outhouse at the edge of the lot. Evie worked in all weather for nine or ten months each year, rain, cold, wind, extreme heat. One winter she posted a picture of herself on Facebook, where she has more than six hundred friends (I have less than one hundred), buried in five or six multicolored layers of wool and fleece. On hot summer days, I thought, the string-like shirt from Paris would be perfect. I lobbed it at her and the shirt unfurled as she caught it.

"This is way too nice for me," she said, adding that her boobs were still sore from the biopsy.

OK, I thought, I'd been wrong. False alarm. The dream state bulletin had been incorrect. "Wear it anyhow," I said. "It'll look great on you. I could never wear a shirt like that."

Where Evie inherited Mom's black Irish beauty, I inherited her rather lumpy arms.

Months later, it was clear Evie was losing weight. Skeletal legs poked out of her shorts. Her swimmer's arms sagged, the flesh crinkled and loose. True, she ran five miles several times a week and swam a mile on days she didn't run. She insisted with listless conviction that she was fine. I kept watch, though. She was decidedly haggard, like someone who was sick.

"Evie, please, go to the doctor again," I nagged. "You're way too thin."

It turned to winter. I wondered if she secretly liked her new boniness.

"I can eat anything. I just don't gain weight," she'd shrug. "The doctor said it could be my metabolism. Besides, I'm still exercising and eating well. It's just my shitty life."

Her "shitty life" was a running joke about the jumble of their house with its outbuildings, chickens, and unfinished remodel.

We find a small table in the back of Papalote. I notice the restroom is nearby and excuse myself to rinse my face in cold water. What has come over me? It's been one hell of a year and now, here we are, next to a neighborhood I've been avoiding for decades. But today was supposed to be all about her, not me. That was another lifetime ago.

Here's what happened: I was part of a co-op that purchased two buildings with five units at the corner of Twenty-Fifth and Noe Streets, an up-and-coming area. I used my divorce settlement to loan my friend Amanda money to buy her unit, and I bought the best of the five apartments for myself. It had two floors with views of Twin Peaks and the Bay. It had great light. It was a fantastic investment, a retirement insurance policy. Then, I lost it when I sold it to two partners for drug money, a pitiful $10,000. It's a long sorry story. I'll spare you the murky details, but it still stings.

"Must have used roasted chiles," Evie says, pressing her lips, working her tongue and palate, savoring the salsa she doused over her burrito. "Not as good as Nopalito, but not bad for a taqueria."

We'd lunched at Nopalito the day she'd had her chemo port removed. During an interrogation of the waitress there, Evie discovered they used chiles from Tierra Vegetables, her farm. She brought food samples home to Wayne.

~~~~~

Some months after her breast cancer false alarm, Evie had a pain in her side that became too persistent to ignore. The first doctor said it was nothing, so she got a second opinion. Tests revealed a mass on the right side: possible ovarian cancer. Ovarian cancer killed two of our aunts. This was just before the Christmas holidays in 2009. Mom's birthday is four days before Christmas, and that year we all gathered on the Central Coast as usual. Paul commented that hugging Evie felt like gathering a bunch of skinny sticks in his arms. She was all bones despite eating as much as she wanted.

"Is she going to be all right?" Johnny asked.

Since Evie and I lived fewer than ten miles apart, I was the default expert on what was happening with her. When our schedules worked out, we'd ride together the three hundred miles from our homes in Sonoma County to Mom's in Morro Bay, talking, listening to music, singing lustily to our favorite Jackson Browne or Bonnie Raitt songs. "Running on Empty" is a cathartic sing-along. That year there was little or no music in the Saab on the drive back home. While Evie scheduled surgery with staff at Kaiser San Francisco from the passenger seat, she kept looking up from her phone as if it were something I should consent to. I drove on, through Gilroy and Morgan Hill, hands, stomach, neck clenched. It was gray outside. By the time we arrived home, her surgery was set for New Year's Eve.

"The sooner the better," I said.

We had a hushed Christmas at the house John and I shared on the western edge of Santa Rosa, near Sebastopol. We all held our breath and struggled to be optimistic. I thought my sister was brave just to show up.

Evie's birthday is four days after Christmas, and like the family jock that she is, she ran fifty-eight minutes on December 29, 2009—one minute for each of her years. That's been her birthday tradition ever since her first marathon in 1999. She drank her pre-op liquids the next day, and early on the morning of the last day of that year, I picked her and Wayne up and headed for the hospital. Wayne sat in front, Evie in back, ashen and nervous, periodically exclaiming, "I hope I don't die."

Bobby had died in a horrific car collision forty years earlier. That night, in 1969, Evie had been working at Carl's Jr. She was six-teen. Maureen had to drive to Carl's to deliver the bad news. Until 2009, Bobby had remained the big deal in our immediate family. We all wore seatbelts and felt we'd been inoculated from further grief. One tragedy per family per lifetime was enough.

I drove to Evie's surgery as if on a delicate mission, carefully, kindly. When we turned off Lombard onto Divisadero, a small light blinked in my consciousness. Divisadero, all the way up and over into Noe Valley—the way to my old house. It had been a safe, direct route when I'd been high. On my personal tour of Places I Bottomed Out, it was a highlight.

Wayne and I found the waiting area while Evie checked in. Wayne is a quiet man, not a talker. We pretty much kept to our-selves during the long wait. Dr. Powell emerged after five hours in surgery. I stood back as she spoke with Wayne, observing his brown eyes grow wide and redden, his face fill with bad news. The surgery had confirmed cancer. The doctor talked about debulking, traces in the omentum and bowel. A bit on the diaphragm. Some of the vocabulary stark in its unfamiliarity. It was not a good prog-nosis. Ovarian cancer is latent, sneaky, and nasty, and there was that family history. Fuck, I thought, as the taste of waiting and too much caffeine met in my jaw and eyes. Had our family's prolonged dispensation from grief finally met its expiration date? I felt that portal unlocking.

The next day Johnny and his partner David brought an iPhone speaker dock so Evie could listen to ocean waves and music, masking the incessant din of the hospital. Johnny signaled me out to the hallway, where he blurted, "It's all over, isn't it, Pats?"

More than twenty years earlier, Evie had helped me get to rehab. I was an embarrassment, and my sister feared a crazy violent boyfriend would kill me. Or I'd overdose. I'd tried once, taking most of a bottle of Valium after a fight with my ex-husband. When I came to, Evie said she'd disown me if I tried that again. Evie's disgust and worry dissipated over my years of sobriety. I slid back into my role of her big sister, the one she admired for her politics and advice and clothes. I dress Evie for special events, often from my own closet. She's wearing my shawl, shirt, and skirt in her wedding picture. She owns just two pair of shoes, running shoes and an ancient pair of Dansko clogs. Evie is tough. When I was working AA's Ninth Step and making amends to her, she didn't say, as many did, "It's all right, Patsy. You weren't that bad. We're glad you're sober now." Instead, she said, "You were an asshole. And pathetic. Glad you're done with that."

Now here she was, subjected to aggressive two-pronged chemotherapy, one intravenous, the other peritoneal. She sat two days for the intravenous, and then for another she lay in a bed while cancer-killing drugs dribbled directly into her abdomen. Each infusion lasted three or four hours, which she spent with visitors, cheerful oncology nurses, on her iPhone, chatting away, unless she was really wiped out. Afterward, she would rest for a week, and the first few days were rough. I brought an occasional meal and went for slow walks with her around a vineyard.

Her thick merle hair fell out in fat chunks. More dismaying than funny, she had a look some punks cultivate, a few lanky hunks hanging off an otherwise bald or shaved head. Finally, a friend came over and finished the job. My sister was bald. On the rare occasion she went out in public, she sported a white bandana with navy blue ties that resembled a skipper cap. She chose this plain triangle from a huge array of colorful scarves and wigs—donations and gifts, plus the supply at the oncology center. There were paisleys, stripes, and more, but this was her favored cap. Wigs didn't suit her. She's earthy, never wears makeup. Her vanity is rare, situational, Spartan. Wearing the ridiculous cap was like an announcement: "Yes! I have cancer, and I'm fighting it, and winning. Fuck cancer." She didn't want pity; she wanted everyone to know that anyone could have cancer.

Papalote is too crowded for much conversation. After we finish, we find ourselves walking around the Mission. I'm hoping for a short stroll, not eager to confront the neighborhood I'd abandoned to an addiction.

"I remember walking to the Mission from your old place," Evie insists. "I'm just sure we did."

"Well, Noe is probably up that way." I point in the vague direction of a hill.

We enter a tchotchkes shop, where the clerk tells us incorrectly that Noe is just three blocks up the hill.

"I already did three miles on the treadmill," I say as we set out.

"And I swam my mile," she counters.

"So, we don't need the exercise." I'm nervous about how I'll react to seeing my old place. I've been a good sister, a grown up. I love spending time with Evie, and she's been so brave. Why cast the shadow of my past on her day of good news?

"Five pounds," Evie pats her belly. "This is for the five pounds we need to lose."

"But it's so steep."

"We can do this," she declares as we face the formidable urban hill. We wonder aloud whether the raised horizontal ridges across the old cement sidewalk are to keep people from falling backward or to break the run downhill.

Evie was a teacher before farming and started running marathons after a student got leukemia. Back in the day, I ran to balance my excesses. If I could run three miles, then I was cool to smoke and drink as much as I chose and do cocaine as available. I'm more of a walker these days. We continue walking, approaching the place on which I squandered my divorce money. The beautiful two-story flat I let slip away.

The little alarms buzzing in my brain grow louder, signaling my nervous system. My heart pumps an ancient hollow ache. Hallucinating across the Bay Bridge after scoring in Alameda, exiting at Army, finding my way to the corner of Twenty-Fifth and Noe. Alone, middle of the night. That was me, doing that.

We trudge up to Dolores. On to Church, past Vicksburg, then Sanchez. I spot the junior high school, and then we're at the corner of Twenty-Fifth and Noe. We turn right and stop at the first house. Lots of concrete, a few anemic trees, the meager school building, nothing of architectural note save a few pastel houses up the block.

"It was almost thirty years ago," I say.

My dog Lulu and I did laps on that junior high track. I existed on a diet of spirulina, red wine, and cocaine.

Evie, in radiant good health, gives me a look.

I'd watched scary people parade up and down Noe into the early morning on their way to the Castro or bars on Twenty-Fourth Street. I'd slept little, cocooned in an obsession. It was a great relief, fitting into skinny pants and not giving a serious shit about anything, weary of being a good Catholic girl. I professed to care about politics and volunteered the living room for a small event for a friend's cause. I darted in the background, glad to be of use, half out of my body. Disconnected. Bottoming.

Now, looking in at the dark passageway of stairs that once led me to my second floor flat, I feel no rush of emotion. I exhale. Yes, the furniture in there was once mine. An orange sofa. A flea market oak table that Evie has now. A gray IBM typewriter. I wonder absurdly if my wedding dress could still be in the basement. I lost track of so much.

"Well, here we are," I say.

"Does it bother you to see it?" Evie asks, tilting her head at a slight angle.

"Not anymore," I sigh. "I'm done with this place. I fucked up and made a mess of things. For years I felt like a failure, losing this goldmine. But I was sick. I had to lose it to be where I am today. To be well. Does that make sense?"

"I think so," she says.

"It had great views though."

We share a quick hug and walk down the hill to my car to make our way across the bridge and home, one of us in remission, the other in recovery.

I knew right where I was.

~~~~~~

Update: Evie has been cancer-free for fourteen years. Spending time on the Central Coast during Mom's decline, she reconnected with her first sweetheart (and ex-husband), Mark. Today, she's a certified Master Gardener and a sourdough mistress in Arroyo Grande. She makes cupcakes for all the local Truxaw birthdays. Evie, Michael, and I walk, hike, and explore San Luis Obispo County's many beaches and parks at least monthly. She texts beforehand to see what variety of homemade sourdough bread we prefer. I usually opt for the olive. Delicioso.

Evie with Wheelie, her birthday gift wheelbarrow in Cayucos, CA. Yes, she loved it enough to name it. December 29, 2017.

Johnny: Raku

Johnny looking out over Long Valley Caldera from Mammoth Mountain. Around 1973.

No relationship in my family has had as much movement, as many mood swings or WTF moments, as the one I've had with Johnny. The graph of our relationship looks like jagged lines. Not too long ago it seemed likely he was out of our lives for good.

Johnny is number six of eight siblings. I'm number two.

He was sixteen when the accident took Bobby's life. He was at home at Janss Way when the call came, and he went with our parents to the hospital on the outskirts of Los Angeles where Bobby was taken. He waited and walked the halls while Mom and Dad went back to where medics worked unsuccessfully to save Bobby. Johnny describes that night as the worst experience of his life. In 2022, he shared an essay with us that he'd written titled "Bobby is Still Around." In it, he writes that the rest of the school year after Bobby died was pretty much a blur. He was uncomforted. Here's a heartbreaking passage:

Up until the funeral, no one had taken me or any of my siblings aside to give us love or care. No one attempted to explain how God could let this happen. My world was completely torn apart.

When I graduated from UC Irvine less than a year after the accident and moved to Washington, DC, for a job, Johnny sent me long, detailed letters. He was the only one of my siblings to do so. He was curious about life in the capital during the rise and fall of Nixon, the Vietnam War, demonstrations, McGovern. He sent maps detailing where he and his friends had gone camping in an Econoline van he'd outfitted for such adventures. He wasn't only curious; he was industrious. He set up a darkroom in the garage to process and print the abundance of photos he took. The first time I came home from DC, he arrived with Mom to pick me up at a friend's house wearing a suit. He was tearful and choked up to see me. He was geeky, gangly, and tall for our family, and he wore dark-rimmed glasses. I had no idea of the depth of his despair and loneliness. He never mentioned it in his letters.

I've written about the aftermath of our brother's death and how the family separately and together dealt with it and didn't. Yet, it's only in recent years that I've heard Johnny lament how much suffering that night caused him, how none of us knew what it was like for him. I'd like to emphasize the word "heard" in the last sentence. We didn't have the language to talk about death and loss and the unexpected isolation from others it creates. Johnny may have been communicating in all kinds of ways, but I only recently began to hear him.

Johnny will tell you he would have become a professional photographer if he'd done what his heart wanted. That, he says, is his passion, his art, his talent. He doesn't believe our parents encouraged us to develop impractical trades, which is probably true. Daddy once told me the most practical class I could take was typing, and he also said pharmacy was a good career for a woman. I don't know whether Johnny went to law school reluctantly. My gut assessment is that he was torn. Much as he wanted to be an artist, he was also capable of—and craved the rewards of—conventional success.

In the late 1970s, Johnny worked during the summers and beyond in the grill at Tuolumne Meadows in Yosemite. It was, and maybe still is, a special, perhaps magical, place for him, a place that fed his spirit. There was a transition period after he graduated from Berkeley and hustled to make a living. During this time, he sold fresh summer fruit, built a beautiful fence along one side of my yard in Oakland, worked at the UC Berkeley library.

He married a woman, went to UC Davis School of Law in the 1980s, lived in Berkeley, and worked for Bay Area cities. By all appearances, he was in the midst of a successful career. When his wife left him for a woman, Johnny was enraged and felt betrayed. That was the first time I saw flashes of intense anger and hurt in him.

Johnny is kind, funny, generous, charismatic. He's sentimental, supportive. He's dispensed free legal advice to family members upon request, and even on occasion unsolicited. Johnny can also be scornful, haughty, rash, impulsive.

He laughed with me in a sunny Healdsburg backyard on July 4, 1987, a few days before I went to rehab. We sat in beach chairs, drinking beer and talking about the family's predisposition to drink, drug, and madness. He was one of two siblings who visited me in treatment in St. Helena. He brought a box of small perfumes from Nordstrom. I still have one of the bottles sitting on my dresser. About a year later he swept into the shabby cottage that was my first solo housing after getting sober, a new microwave under his arm. "Where should I put this?" he asked, setting it down on the kitchen counter. He'd show up in Healdsburg to take Evie and me for a ride when he got a new car. First it was a bland Ford Taurus, later a convertible Volvo, Jackson Browne's "In the Shape of a Heart" blasting forth.

Over the years, Johnny and I exchanged special gifts, a signed Evans raku ceramic pot from me, a chili pepper necklace from him. Whenever I visited his homes in Sausalito, Oakland, or Orinda, I'd look for the raku vase and find it displayed in his spare modern living rooms. It became a check-in point for me.

We also exchanged complicit insights into our dysfunctional family. We had what I considered a special bond, an unspoken respect and acceptance. Maybe he thought I was smart, and I knew he was.

But did we ever talk about Bobby? Not that I remember. He would share some of his love life with me. I met a few of his friends and partners. From the back seat of my hot VW Fox, heading to our nephew Bobby's first wedding in Bakersfield, I heard about how he longed for a relationship.

As the only lawyer, the rest of us teachers, or in Paul's case a salesman, Johnny became the most well-off. He emerged as the de facto big brother, intentionally or not, filling the gap Bobby left. He was successful, good-looking, a bit (sometimes a lot) confident and cocky.

Johnny with Maureen at Bobby and Katie's wedding. Summer 2008.

Johnny was in his early forties when Daddy died in 1995. He made the arrangements and paid for almost everything. Daddy died in Morro Bay, but his funeral and burial were in Orange County. Johnny booked those of us no longer living there, which was most of us, into a hotel. He dealt with the funeral homes in both counties, and the cemetery. I remember feeling amazed, relieved, and grateful.

At some point after the divorce from his wife, Johnny came out as gay. He had two long-term relationships that I'm aware of. At least one of them ended suddenly. "I'm done with him," he announced, having kicked the man out. Several years later, when he was working as an attorney for the City of Oakland, he met handsome and deaf David. David worked for Deaf Communication Services. They fell in love, Johnny learned ASL (American Sign Language), and David became an enchanting addition to the family. He or Johnny would often arrange for an interpreter to be present at gatherings. Some family members already knew sign language. Evie took a class. I tried unsuccessfully, but we made it work. David has a remarkable ability to focus, making him a wicked competitor at Rummikub games. Johnny pronounced their marriage in 2013 the happiest day of his life.

When Mom fell and broke her hip in February 2009, she was a healthy ninety-two years old, and we siblings circled around and showed up to help her. Text messages, emails, phone calls, and miles tore up and down the state. It was a big deal that the woman who'd had the greatest influence over our lives was down. Even so, I was struck at the time by Johnny's intense emotionality.

"This is the beginning of the end, isn't it, Pats?" he wailed, calling me one night while on the beach near Mom's Morro Bay home. It must've been windy because it sounded like he was heading into a storm. Soon, he seemed to expect control of most aspects of her care. As a lawyer (and one of the boys), he'd been designated with Paul as Mom's medical power of attorney. Evie and I had researched long-term and home-care options and costs, and when we advocated applying for the financial assistance Mom was qualified for, he vehemently dismissed our suggestion.

"Not Welfare Mama!" He declared. "She's too good for that!"

My husband John, who did construction for a living, helped with modifications to Mom's house so she could return home from extended care. Johnny got nasty about John's recommendations for safety adaptions. In that conversation he frenetically repeated, "John does not have a vote! John does not have a vote!" while clanging dishes in his kitchen. I found myself with one hand over my heart, the other holding the phone away from my ear, letting the rant wind down. What had happened to my brother? What had happened to Johnny?

I got that he was probably going through anticipatory grief, but as Mom progressed into dementia, we all were. Mom's funds were being exhausted, and Johnny wasn't being realistic. Verbal digs from the ridiculous to the vulgar continued.

I tried to analyze and understand why he was so angry with me. I prayed for him and talked to my sponsor and therapist. I did not want to believe Johnny was being his real self, and he wasn't consistently temperamental and disparaging. When he and David were together his charm and charisma reappeared. He'd be kind, curious, and generous: If we were out for a meal he invariably picked up the check. Once Mom could no longer stay at home, he was the one who dealt with the long-term care business office, utilizing resources Evie and I had suggested earlier.

The day after Mom died on August 1, 2014 (her decline lasting five years), we gathered for lunch at Dorn's in Morro Bay, and Johnny ordered a bottle of Champagne. I put my hand over the flute as the pouring went around the outdoor table, indicating I'd pass. I'm in recovery, after all.

"You can have one drink to toast your mother!" Johnny sneered while waving a glass under my nose. Someone told him to stop.

There's more to this part of the story, and for the record I've participated in plenty of non-alcoholic toasts in my sober years. It's been hard to separate and sort out my reactions to his pointed jabs from the jabs themselves. Yes, they were hurtful, and thankfully I had help shielding myself from them and him. I'd learned not to fight back or engage with him. Our mother had just died, and we were entering a new stage of mourning.

I've been both blessed and cursed to be an observer of the big story that is playing out in my life. Something was not right with Johnny. What had happened to my brother? That question again. We're all high-wired and on edge in our family group, and at times his fragile wiring frayed and shorted out in caustic, self-protective ways.

For a few years after Mom's passing, he was mainly mellow and appeared content in his marriage to David, his work, their home, and life. I continued to check for the raku vase on the mantlepiece or hearth when I was (rarely) at their house, a reassurance that at heart we were okay.

After John and I moved from Sonoma County down the coast to Los Osos, Johnny, David, and the rest of the family visited several times. Evie, Michael, and Marguerite also live in San Luis Obispo County, which made it a convenient spot to gather. When the

COVID-19 pandemic arrived in 2020, we began holding monthly family Zoom meetings on Sundays. It was crazy good fun when all nineteen of us were there. We joked about one another's lockdown hair, Paul wore costumes, and one of the kids, Jacob, told knock-knock and other jokes.

Then, just as the COVID years were easing up, Johnny began having mini seizures. A worried David called me through a deaf interpreter and asked me to talk to him. When I got Johnny on the phone, his acerbic edge was absent. He was worried, having brief episodes like blackouts or phase outs. He went to a neurologist and kept in touch. Then, months later, kaboom! Explosion! A hysterical, hyper-ventilating Johnny called to say he was leaving David. He was enraged when we checked in with David, our brother-in-law.

It was a hellish time that culminated in a downward spiral and reactive and rash behavior. Here's a partial list:

- selling their home
- getting a divorce
- being diagnosed with a form of epilepsy
- buying a condo in Sausalito
- getting a fancy bicycle and riding around the Golden Gate National Recreation Area (GGNRA), including the Golden Gate Bridge
- selling his car
- walking, riding, and taking lots of photos, some of them excellent, which he shared to a list that for a while included Evie and me
- emphasizing how happy he was
- emailing cousins to say he no longer had a family, citing his inventory of disappointments and injuries
- accusing us (everyone but Marguerite) of being a cabal
- re-finding God
- informing Paul, Evie, Michael, and me that we'd been disowned
- amending his trust so the city of Sausalito or the GGNRA were beneficiaries rather than his nieces and nephews

There was more—a lot more—but you get the idea. It was exhausting, laughable, and painful. I prayed he wouldn't get killed riding his bike on that busy bridge. When I asked who his emergency contact was, he said it was God. My conclusion, or assessment, or whatever the correct word might be, was (and is) that Johnny is a seventy-year-old man with a vulnerable sixteen-year-old kid inside still yearning to be comforted. My nonprofessional diagnosis is that he'd yet to process and understand what happened to him and the rest of us when his older brother died. He'd repressed his confusion and grief over that sudden loss for years, and so subsequent losses (like his first marriage ending, Mom's death, and doubts about David's faithfulness) were triggering. His young adolescent self was still seeking comfort, and so he broke and blew up his life.

There was a period of peace and quiet. When Paul would ask whether anyone had heard from Johnny, I could say no and feel some relief in that answer. So, when I saw Johnny's name pop up on my phone in late June 2022, I momentarily froze and let him leave a message. His voice on the recording sounded calm. He inquired about the trust account I manage for Marguerite. When I called him back, it was cordial, pleasant. A few days later, my sober anniversary approaching, I sent him a text and asked whether he recalled sitting with me in the sun that weekend before I went into the St. Helena Recovery Center. I thanked him for being there that day. It had meant a lot to me. I don't think he remembered, but his reply was kind.

At the end of July 2022, he sent Paul, Evie, Michael, and me an apology email, writing:

I realize now that I was an asshole in sending the letters I sent to you all last year. I think we all have a lot to offer each other in our lives, and so if you are up to it, please accept this apology and let me know if you are up to discussing life's ups and downs. love, Johnny

Over the next twenty-four hours we all accepted his apology and released a restrained and cautious sigh of relief. John and I visited him in Sausalito on our drive back to Los Osos from Christmas in Sonoma County. He was kind, nervous. I almost didn't recognize him in the thin, bearded man dashing across the parking lot to greet us. We had a short and, for me, poignant visit. I didn't see evidence of the raku vase during the brief time I was in his condo. The space looked barely lived in. He bought us sandwiches for the road at Mollie Stone's, where he said he got all his dinners.

A few months later, Johnny called to share that he'd started hearing voices. They were, and presumably still are, telling him he isn't a good person. "After I get off the phone, a voice will probably say, 'She sounds like a nice person, but you're an asshole.'" From what he described then, the voices don't tell him to do anything; rather, they judge him. The voices are so distracting he can't drive. His psychiatrist says it isn't schizophrenia, which our sister Marguerite has, and which runs in our dysfunctionally wired gene pool. Johnny's anger seemed to have evaporated. It feels cruel that it may have turned on him. He's become perplexed, resigned, afraid he's lost his charm (I've assured him he hasn't).

He and David resumed talking and meeting on Zoom. David visited him when Johnny turned seventy at the end of April 2023.

In October of 2023, Johnny tried to hurt himself, which resulted in placement in a small psychiatric hospital in Sacramento where he was safe and seen by an excellent mental health team, including a therapist and psychiatrist. Unfortunately, that same support and luxury of inquiry doesn't extend into the outside world of mental health care.

He now lives in a senior community in Sacramento. Annie, our niece, lives and works in Sacramento and has been a source of cheer and support. He spends time watching tennis and other sports on TV, going for long walks, and socializing with fellow residents during meals. This season, he's joined our family fantasy football league. He's an integral part of several family text chats, and he's on the phone with one or some of us frequently. He continues suffering from auditory hallucinations. There's a slim possibility he'll relocate to the Central Coast—he surely would if obtaining medical care here weren't such an obstacle.

As for the raku vase, I asked while he was packing to move from Sausalito to Sacramento if he still had it. He didn't know what I was talking about. I've learned that giving it to him meant more to me than wherever it's ended up. There's a tenderness in Johnny, and in all of us, that needs to be witnessed and protected so we can love ourselves and be whole.

<div align="center">~~~~~~</div>

What do we learn from this story about my brother Johnny?

Watch out for the crisscross of genetics and grief.

Don't ignore the depth, mystery, and blessings of grief. Forgive yourself and others for ignorance and ineptness in dealing with emotional wounds. Face your genetics. Our family has bad, very bad, wiring. We inherited mental illness, alcoholism, addiction. That is fact. Get help.

We also inherited some glue that's stuck us together, and the smarts and heart to do something about the other stuff. Talk to one another. Ask for the truth.

My advice to anyone reading this: Do it sooner rather than later. Therapy works. Counseling helps. If a family member suffers a loss, don't expect them to just get over it. We all process grief differently. I have no doubt that if my brother had been given (or taken) the option of counseling or therapy when he was younger, he would be a different and happier man today. Is it too late for him to heal? Will he forever cling to that worst day of his life? I don't know, but I'm cautiously optimistic. He's slowly getting better, working on it, and he's not alone.

Our collective brain was severely tested, but it's resilient. We don't give up on one another, no matter how sideways one of us goes.

Forgiveness is huge. Reconciliation happens.

Marguerite: Beautiful One

At the outset of a weeklong family gathering at Newport Beach, Marguerite had a meltdown. It was the week between Christmas and New Year's in 2015, more than a full year after Mom's death and the first time since her burial that we'd gathered. Why did Marg decompensate when it had been her suggestion that we get together in Newport?

She's the seventh of eight children in the family, the fourth girl. She was tagged "the beautiful one" early on because of her wavy white-blonde hair and sweet countenance. The nickname stuck as she grew tall and graceful. She was twelve years old when Bobby died, and she and Michael were left at home to experience first-hand the residue and atmosphere of our parents' long grieving. Michael has said that Mom and Daddy took care of the basics with the two of them but that they had virtually no supervision or special attention. Whether and how this period contributed to their future selves is open to question.

Marguerite delivering birthday cake to Mom at Janss Way. Around 1968.

When Marguerite was a student at UC Berkeley in 1980, she began to think her English professor had moved inside her head. For me, that was the first alarming indicator about our youngest sister's state of mind. She stayed with me for a short time in 1980 or 1981, after my first husband, Mark, moved out. I'm fuzzy as to why she came, but it's possible Mom arranged it because she and Daddy were worried about her. What I remember is that she wasn't like the cheerful sister I'd known: She was quiet and preoccupied. Still, she was only twenty-four. She seemed to me like a young person between things. Marguerite went home to Morro Bay after her stay with me (though she may have gone back to Berkeley first). I was distracted with a divorce, work, and moving from Oakland to San Francisco.

With ten years' difference in our ages, we'd never been close sister siblings. Marguerite was, and is, an adventurer. She was tall and graceful and silly. I'm not clear on the exact order of events, but Marguerite was completing an English degree from Berkeley. (She'd been to school in Oregon prior to that.) Even after her symptoms started, she managed to get a job as an au pair in Paris. When she returned, she worked in a law office in San Luis Obispo. She continued to exhibit symptoms and was diagnosed, as I recall, as paranoid schizophrenic. My parents got her involved with support services through the county, which included medication, socialization, case management, and more.

Marguerite resisted treatment and acceptance of her disease with a magnificent imagination that has flared up periodically over the years. She's had an affinity for hopping on planes, trains, and buses, and for slipping away before she can be stopped. On at least one occasion she made it all the way to the East Coast and was heading for a return to Paris before our parents intercepted her. I must admit I was both happy and proud of her for getting as far away as she did. Once he got her home, Daddy nailed the front door shut so she couldn't leave. I find it hard to believe he really did this, but I have an image of the boards crisscrossed over the locked door, and I can hear him sputtering and pounding while some of us wondered who the crazy person is. Marguerite confirms that Daddy did in fact nail the front door shut.

We have our share of alcoholics, addicts, neurotics, and undiagnosed bipolars, but Marguerite is the only certified paranoid schizophrenic besides Auntie Carol, Daddy's sister. We loved Carol, who was sweet and quirky. Daddy many times rushed out of the house to rescue, calm down, or otherwise intervene with his sister. Intervention sometimes meant having her hospitalized. I can't vouch for the others, but I know I prayed I wouldn't turn out like Carol. The notion that our gorgeous Marguerite inherited this trait was unfathomable and infuriating to me. It still is.

Where Carol was meek, Marguerite is extravagant. She's disarming, smart, industrious, occasionally frightening, wild, angry, suspicious, and worrying. She's also grateful, humble, careless, curious, and endearing. Many adjectives describe her behavior and diagnosis. The standard definition according to VeryWell Mind is as follows: "Paranoid schizophrenia is characterized by predominantly positive symptoms of schizophrenia, including delusions and hallucinations. These debilitating symptoms blur the line between what is real and what isn't, making it difficult for the person to lead a typical life." The "positive symptoms" are identifiable experiences such as auditory and visual hallucinations, paranoia, and delusions.[7]

After her diagnosis, Marguerite mostly lived at home with Mom and Daddy. She went through periods of stability during which she worked in job programs supervised by the county. For a while she decorated terracotta pots with small tiles that she gave away as gifts and then began selling at the Saturday Morro Bay Farmers Market. She painted and kept (may still keep) a journal. She was protected by Mom for years and thrived while living at home where she didn't have to pay rent and had the constant support and love of both parents. Mom continued to protect and support her after Daddy died.

When Mom fell and broke her hip in 2009, Michael returned to Morro Bay from Oregon to help care for her. He and Marg made an increasingly difficult combination. Her idiosyncrasies coupled with Mom's increased needs pushed his buttons. Evie and I helped her get into Transitions[8] housing around the same time Mom moved into a long-term care facility. All these changes,

---

7   "Positive Symptoms in Schizophrenia: Hallucinations, Delusions, Disorganized Thinking, Abnormal Motor Activity," VeryWell Mind, accessed February 15, 2025, https://www.verywellmind.com/positive-symptoms-in-schizophrenia-2953124.

8   Transitions-Mental Health Association, accessed February 15, 2025, https://www.t-mha.org.

compounded by physical ailments, slowly contributed to a setback in Marguerite's relative stability. She moved from one Transitions house to another, enrolled at Cuesta College, and got A's and B's in child development classes. She finally got a subsidized apartment in San Luis Obispo and a cat. She's had broken bones and other health crises, including one when she didn't get her daily meds. The ignorance and lack of proper care for the severely mentally ill in some institutions is deplorable, not to mention the neglect, and we've learned to advocate for her in such situations.

After Mom died in August 2014, Marguerite suggested she'd really like to go to Newport, where the family beach house used to be. We'd occasionally rent a place after the beach house was sold so our troops could gather on familiar and beloved surf and sand. The prospect of spending a week on the oceanfront appealed to all of us, and so Evie and our niece Annie and I put together a plan to make it happen. A few of our clan opted for a hotel, and others lived nearby. The rest of us spent the week after Christmas 2015 in a large oceanfront rental; there were nineteen of us present most days.

The energy on the first day was loud and jubilant, the day outside sunny, bright, and cool. As I recall, everyone was looking good and happy to see one another. That is, until Marguerite launched into a blood-curdling outburst.

She'd been quiet at first and had probably become progressively anxious as more family arrived. In retrospect, I understand that she was triggered, but it wasn't typical of her behavior at that time, so it was confusing when she erupted with a fierce growl. She started in on Johnny, traveling back to childhood and accusing him of breaking her baton with murderous-sounding vehemence in a voice not her own.

Oh great, I thought. *After all the work setting this up, in part because Marguerite said she wanted to do this, our week is already ruined.*

Once it started, the voice or voices in her head fed her paranoia, and the decibels and intensity increased. Her eyes were wild and mean. I felt a weary despair. *What if someone calls the police?*

Where was the quiet Marguerite who had nodded off in the back seat of my car as I drove her and Mom to Anaheim countless times in the past? Where was the mellow Marg making tamale pie for dinner in the kitchen at Morro Bay? Or the artistic one, selling her multicolored tiled pots?

"But Marg, you wanted to be here. Take a breath. You're scaring the children." I attempted to intervene.

"You take a breath!" she growled. "You take a breath, Patsy. You're not the ruler of everything!" And she ran out of the living room and down the hall to her bedroom.

Was she wishing like the rest of us that she'd never gotten wound up? That she could rewind this whole scene? That whatever had triggered her hadn't so successfully summoned her demons? Was she the unfortunate recipient of accumulated family demons, the sensitive receptacle of unspoken resentments and fears? Likely all the above ran through her mind, as it did mine.

Paul's daughter, my niece Erin, who at the time was becoming a special education teacher, went after Marguerite, gently knocking on the door and quietly asking if she could come in. Erin calmed her aunt down and, for the first few days at the beach, made a point to check in with and soothe and amuse her. Erin saved the week for all of us. Marguerite mostly kept to herself and made it through, even going into the cold January ocean for a short swim. Erin has a huge heart, and Marguerite clearly holds a special place in it. Marg got herself together. She joined us for group photos on our last night.

On her insistence, Marguerite moved out of supervised housing into an apartment on her own. Evie and I didn't think she should leave the professional support, but Marguerite insisted she was ready. She had more dramatic eruptions, something that had never plagued her when she'd lived at home with Mom.

John and I moved to Los Osos in early 2017, and Evie and I started attending some of the weekly family support groups Transitions offers. It took us too long to figure out that Marguerite is triggered by family, some members more than others, and by crowds. And that she'd deteriorated without the stability of living with Mom.

~~~~~~

In September 2017, Marguerite went missing. Missing to the extent that we resorted to filing a police report. Amtrak records helped locate her in Santa Fe, New Mexico. She'd been to an art workshop there several years earlier, but this time she wound up in a homeless shelter. Her phone battery died. Eventually I located and was able to speak with a kind counselor who relayed a message for Marg to call us, which she finally did. It was late enough in September that it was starting to get cold there. I arranged for a ticket home, and Evie agreed to pick her up at the train station. We didn't know for certain whether she would be on the train until she got off. People with her diagnosis don't keep in touch with family, don't return phone calls, and are often suspicious or indifferent.

Once she was back, Marguerite and I met at Ascendo Coffee Shop across from the apartment building where she was living in downtown San Luis Obispo. We chatted comfortably about books, family, and goals. She conceded she'd never become a lay missionary, and I said I'd never write the great American novel. She said she'd like to take library science. I complimented her on the heavy New Mexico–style sweater she wore. She smiled sheepishly and admitted she'd gotten it at the homeless shelter in Santa Fe. We both paused and then laughed. It's moments like this when I not only love but am delighted by my sister.

I now have primary responsibility for managing Marguerite's Special Needs Trust, which was set up in our parents' trust specifically for her. This management has necessitated several straight-talk meetings at Ascendo about her spending habits. She used to regularly call, desperate for me to rush into San Luis Obispo to pay her phone bill. At least once I had to cover her rent. She'd had no money left to buy groceries.

"You're just trying to control me," she'd hiss. "I'm going to sue you for not giving me my money."

There was at least a kernel of truth in what she said. On occasion I had to get up and leave to avoid a full-on outburst at a coffeehouse. She wasn't happy with me, and it was a tough part to play. But it was the right thing to do. I prayed for her, and for the ability to be patient and communicate better. Eventually we came to a peaceful solution. Over time, Marguerite and I discovered subjects to talk about besides money: books we were reading, what she'd like to study, what I was doing.

John and I had moved from Sonoma County to the Central Coast to be closer to family and to help Evie support Marguerite, who despite her protestations needs lots of assistance. I realized I'd need assistance if I ever wanted to have an occasionally successful and realistic relationship with my sister. I knew I had to stop judging and comparing her to "normal" people. Crowds and some family members obviously beckoned her dark side, releasing voices that weren't hers—angry, accusatory, hurt. The family support group and staff at Transitions were a big help, a comfort, a sounding board, and a reality check. I learned to do things small with her, and while I have no recollection of what John and I did on Christmas Day 2017, I do remember Christmas Eve with Marguerite.

Marguerite was getting off the bus as I turned the car around across from the Pine Street transit stop. She didn't notice me at first and wasn't looking as though she expected someone to be there. But I thought I saw her spirit lift when I called out and she noticed me. She wore the cashmere beret I gave her for Christmas in 2015, the year she'd had the blowout in Newport.

She had a couple of bags, including the tatty, blue cloth one she took everywhere. Its contents held papers, documents, and receipts—security she relied on. Her faded rose-colored Land's End coat was well used and looked ripe for replacement. She got in the car, depositing the bags and her cane near her feet. I reminded her to pull on her seatbelt, and we headed out for the short uphill drive to our house. She thanked me for picking her up. So far so good. Soon we were pulling into the driveway. It was Christmas Eve and her first visit to our new home in Los Osos.

She wasn't dressed for a small dinner party, and neither was I. I was nervous to have her over. Nonetheless, John and I were in common cause about making the dinner special and staying calm. I gave her a quick tour of the house. She ventured out to the deck outside the dining room but didn't want to go all the way down to the yard. She seemed to like our simple, small house and took her place in the large chair across from the Christmas tree, which she admired. I asked if she wanted something to drink and brought her mineral water. She agreed to some snacks, so I set her up with some cheese and crackers and a bit of candy.

"Is this Brie?" she asked about a local Brie-like cheese.

She seemed at ease with the offerings and attention, and it felt more easygoing than I'd dared to hope was possible. Belle, our young chocolate Lab, was at her hand frequently, hovering, doting, and dear. Marg patted her on the head and talked quietly to her. They established a natural affinity.

We'd set a nice table, and the meal was festive. I found I just wanted to give her things. So did John. We enjoyed Marguerite for about three hours. She liked the pajamas I gave her and went home with leftover New York strip roast, potatoes, cookies, bread, and candy. John gave her a ride, and she allowed him to walk her upstairs and help with her stuff. She told him she ought to clean up her apartment so she could get a small dog. It was a wonderfully successful dinner and Christmas Eve, so successful it became a tradition we enjoyed for three years until the 2020 pandemic interrupted it. That year and the next we delivered the meal to her.

Marguerite has been learning not to accept invitations if she's not feeling up to socializing. We've had her birthday two years in a row outside at Giuseppe's, down the street from her apartment. I've learned to include a caveat with invitations: if she feels up to it. This year we had John's birthday celebration at Giuseppe's, and she texted at the last minute to say she wouldn't make it and wished us a good time.

There was a period during my early sobriety when I was angry I was an alcoholic and shouldn't ever drink again. I'd become overly fond of strong red and dry, slightly nutty white wines. Pinot Noir, Merlot, Sauvignon Blanc. I realize my former wine preferences probably date me. I had a hard time at first visiting family or going to the unavoidable party where wine was served. A friend recommended a book about the brain and connections between addiction and mental illness. I've searched for the title but can't find it. That book planted a seed connecting dopamine, addiction, self-medication, and schizophrenia. (I use the terms "alcoholism" and "addiction" interchangeably.) I started seeing Gregory, an amazing Buddhist therapist, who seemed to understand me and addiction. With his guidance and energy, I gained perspective on and more acceptance of my alcoholism. He described sobriety as a container that would hold me if I filled it with good stuff, like the Steps, meetings, exercise, meditation. I had to do my part to keep that container whole and healthy. That analogy has worked for me ever since.

Eventually I realized how lucky I was to have the drunk gene, not the schizophrenic one. My genetic inheritance is manageable. My suffering is now my choice. I stopped feeling sorry for myself. I stopped resenting those who could drink without the consequences I experienced. Our family has bad wiring. Marguerite can and does take medication for her disease. It lessens the cruel symptoms, but they never completely go away.

I've developed deep sympathy and respect for my sister. She's one of the bravest people I know. What she's had to give up and live with is a curse. It must've been so perplexing, incomprehensible, when it began presenting itself. She looks troubled and distracted in photos from her early twenties. If you'll pardon the expression, Marguerite, who's ten years younger than I, got the shit gene in our family. She studies, takes online classes, has wanted to be a lay missionary, worked on a library assistant certificate.

Marguerite with niece Annie Sherlock at my marriage celebration to John in Santa Rosa, CA. August 2006.

She has volunteered at Woods Animal Shelter, goes to Mass, learns languages. Marguerite has given me an opportunity to practice and understand unconditional love.

Thanks, Marguerite. We're looking forward to more Christmases with you.

~~~~~~~~

Update: Marguerite spent part of Christmas Day 2023 with us. Due to renovations in her San Luis Obispo housing, she and some other tenants were moved to new apartments in Nipomo, farther away from our home. On Christmas, Michael, who along with Evie is one of her caregivers, drove from Morro Bay to pick Marguerite up and bring her over to our house. We had a lovely day. Later, John and I drove her home.

Michael: The Port

For Michael and Chance

Michael was born just days before Kennedy was elected president in November 1960. I was in the eighth grade at St. Boniface, our parish grammar school, and smitten from the start. I remember him as a loud, talkative, curious child, dark-haired and busy. Mom was almost forty-four when he was born, her last baby. He was doted on by us girls; Evie finally had another dark-haired sibling. I changed his diapers. I helped him learn to read and use the encyclopedia, from which he learned about the Vietnam War and much more. He had a streak of mischief, which in my recollection was more disarming and amusing than troublesome. He was called "Little Mikey" by some of us and "Little Man" by Mom.

Michael was eight years old going on nine when Bobby died. Someone saw him wandering the hallway crying and looking forlorn and lost. When we were in Ireland in 1973, he started wearing a tweed Irish cap that made him look like a junior reporter. He's told me he felt neglected by our parents after Bobby was gone, that they just did the basics. I mentioned this in the chapter on Marguerite already but repeat it here because he's the one who made the point of sharing this with me.

As written elsewhere in the book, Michael moved with our parents to Morro Bay in the summer prior to starting his senior year at Morro Bay High School. He began college at Cal Poly in San Luis Obispo and worked as a waiter at a local upscale restaurant while living at home. He was good at the job, made new friends, garnered lots of tips, and bought a Volvo sportscar. He lost interest in school and began to worry Mom and Daddy. He started to go off the rails.

I happened to be visiting in Morro Bay over his twenty-first birthday in November 1981, at which time both of us were secretly (from our parents) besotted with cocaine. I remember Mom being half-crazed when he left to go out with friends, terrified he wouldn't live through the occasion. (I probably asked him to score drugs for me.) Michael was reckless, and Mom struggled to stay in her skin while anxiously waiting and praying for him to be safe, especially the night after his twenty-first birthday. How hard we were on our parents! True, he became a scoundrel and a rogue, at times an obnoxious drunk. But he had (and has) a thoughtful side. The Christmas before I admitted I was an alcoholic, he nursed me with tea and brandy during a painful bout of tonsillitis. That my younger brother procured me cocaine is in my gallery of shame.

Michael grew into a striking, dark-Irish man and was encouraged to try modeling. Instead, he found drugs and booze. It was after he left his second attempt at recovery (both, as I recall, in the 1980s, neither of them voluntary, both financed by our parents) that Michael met up with Richard Chance Brown outside a bar in either Oakland or San Francisco. Around 1984, they settled in the Russian River area where both my sister Evie and I lived. Those years are sketchy. Michael had by then estranged himself from most of the family. He'd lifted the family silver.

In a memory from the summer of 1984, Chance was walking across the yard at Mill Creek, in the country outside Healdsburg, carrying what appeared to be an assault rifle. Chance had erect posture. I always thought he looked like an Israeli soldier, handsome in a non-American way. Michael walked behind his lover like a manservant, I thought then. I realize now he was in a new relationship, a gay relationship, something he'd had no example for in our family. My brother's partner, whom I'd met just weeks before, was protecting me. It was the morning after Kit, my boyfriend at the time, had sent me to the ER with a gash to my forehead. There'd been a heat wave. We'd both been drunk, Kit drunker than me, as usual. I got stitches and an embarrassing warning from a doctor not to "live like that." You better get out, he said. Chance wanted Kit to get the message that if he messed with me again, he knew how to use the rifle. Before long Kit and I were dancing with Michael and Chance at Fife's, the Russian River's once-popular gay resort.

The guys moved a lot in a short period of time. They moved to Healdsburg, bringing us plants, t-shirts, bottles of wine. Chance introduced me to drinking in the morning. I thought maybe they'd stick around, but they left Healdsburg in the dark of night, bad boys who'd fleeced a friendly winery, which, charmed by their put-together exteriors and clever talk, had hired the pair to host their tasting room.

They were away for a year or two, during which time I got sober. They both masked virulent drunks inside their good looks. How many black eyes did they give one another? After a while I had to ask Michael not to call if he was loaded. Then he called on his birthday, drunk and bewildered. This call was different. Chance was sick. He and Chance had fought, and he was crying, practically hysterical. I'd finally realized preaching did no good, that sending an AA Big Book had been a waste of money. He wasn't ready for that message. He was too lost to go eat, so I ordered a pizza and had it delivered to him, long before DoorDash.

Weeks later Chance called and told me he was *that* sick. Like a tsunami, his T-cell count had crashed. It was officially AIDS. He didn't know if Michael could handle it. Chance's mother Betty bought a property in the countryside outside Portland and put a pretty prefab house on it. The boys had a place for their dog Mercedes, and flowers, and furniture.

When I took the train to visit Michael and Chance in 1991, it was with grave apprehension. I hadn't seen them in several years, our contact mainly tumultuous phone calls. They met me at the train station in their open-air Suzuki jeep. It was warm, summer. I stayed at their place, and we went to Sauvie Island for flowers, listened to music, and made trips into town for Chance's infusions. They still loved to shop, so we shopped, only now they were shopping for food and home furnishings instead of booze and drugs. They displayed their nice things, some no doubt stolen. They were partial to Meier & Frank, where Chance had worked. Their dog Mercedes was a small Aussie mix, lively and obviously much loved. They cooked dinner together. No one was drinking. Chance's illness had calmed things down.

The nurses in the treatment room at the hospital teased and joked with them with familiarity and affection. Chance had a catty shriek of a laugh, a blaze of white-blond hair, a wicked humor. Michael grew tender and watchful. The nurses taught him how to do Chance's home treatments. During that visit I noted how the interior landscape of their lives was changing while their medical vocabulary increased. The port was the dock the drugs go in—into his, Chance's, body. It was a plastic appliance he showed off. It protruded, a plastic hump beneath the clavicle of his narrow chest.

T-cell count. Acyclovir. IV trolley. The latter they decorated with ties, belts, scarves, mobile art. It was suitable for long hanging things, and for Foscarnet, an antiviral drug. The refrigerator, guest room closet, even the bathroom, were repositories for a bizarre collection of white and clear and plastic items: gauze, tubes, needles, and pads, all in boxes and bundles. And of course, the red pail. The one with the skull and crossbones and the black lid with the small opening where the hazardous wastes go.

"I like not drinking," Chance told me. "Not so sure Michael can take it, but I can."

Chance, Michael, and Mercedes at home outside Portland, OR. Summer 1991.

I was inclined to believe him, but Evie said she always had to wonder if they were lying. I'd always had an open place in my heart for Michael, and later for Chance, despite their proclivity for petty crime.

Michael bravely held the bio bucket in the back seat of the jeep as Chance, blind by then in one eye, drove without benefit of a license (it had been at least a year) down the winding rural road and into Portland to exchange the full one for an empty. Let's repeat this. The *bio bucket*. The bio bucket was related to the port where my youngest brother inserted the drugs, all in service of keeping Chance alive as long as possible.

The summer of 1991 was an unexpected lesson in true love for me. From unlikely sources? Who am I to talk? Michael hugging the bio bucket, changing Chance's IVs, handling his partner with love, care, and precision.

I have a photo of Michael, Chance, and Mercedes sitting on their front steps that I took before I left. They have their arms around each other's shoulders. Michael is smiling and looks young and healthy. Chance looks resolved, settled, shoulder to shoulder with my brother. You can't see the port beneath his sleeveless summer shirt.

Michael and Chance and Mercedes relocated from Portland to Cayucos, just north of Morro Bay, to be near the family. Chance lived until early June 1993. Michael took impeccable care of him until the end. He's had ups and downs since then. He went back to Portland for a few years, returning to Morro Bay after Mom broke her hip. He worked for a long time at a local health agency and cared for Mom.

These days he appears firmly single and somewhat solitary. We're baseball fans in our family, and Michael is staunchly in the Dodgers camp. We've gone to a few games together; he treated me once. We even took a mini vacation to Los Angeles to attend a Giants/Dodgers game. I think that's when we talked about what it was like for him and Marguerite to be in the house after Bobby died with the rest of us gone.

"We basically raised ourselves," he said.

I was surprised and horrified that I'd never considered what it was like for them and how that atmosphere may have contributed to their future development.

Michael is super bright, like Marguerite, but like most of us he's had challenges and troubles, including a few more stints in rehab. It's no secret I believe the family disease is corrosive unless a long-term and supported solution is embraced.

In the summer of 2023, after two trips to the ER for extreme intoxication, Michael agreed to go into treatment, which Evie and Johnny financed. Something changed that time. When we walk, which he and Evie and I do regularly, he's the first to arrive at the meeting place, and often with cookies. His white chocolate macadamia nut ones are to die for. He makes the cupcakes for Evie's birthdays and shares his new and favorite recipes with photos. He's typically the guide when the terrain is rough, and he watches out for us. He's the family expert on movies and TV.

In the last year he's become one of Marguerite's caregivers, along with Evie, an arrangement that works well for Marguerite. Michael is good with her, thoughtful and direct, and knows when it's time to walk away. He spends time with Marg playing cards and takes her to doctor's appointments. He's a first-rate brother: observant, caring, and sarcastic. He walked our dogs when I was away once and has a backup key to our house. We share recipes and books and scores.

When Johnny was visiting with our niece Annie over Easter 2024, Michael, who has a history of avoiding and excusing himself from some family gatherings, participated fully, just like he did when Paul visited the Central Coast with two of his children and a grandchild. There's so much baseball and sports talk (and text chat) when the boys (and some girls too) are all together. Johnny commented on how quick-witted Michael is. He beats the hell out of us girls on *The New York Times Spelling Bee* almost daily. He's a master of sharp snark and insights, and his self-deprecating humor is stand-up quality. Wish I could recall one of his recent bits, but my memory is exhausted. Like Johnny, Michael has joined the family fantasy football league, and his average is much higher than mine. So is his memory.

Not to sound mawkish, which he would hate, but it's a gift having him around. As of this writing, Michael, we've yet to buy burner phones.

Michael on the ferry in San Francisco Bay returning from a Giants vs. Dodgers game. Michael bought the tickets, and the Dodgers won. October 1, 2015.

Mom Evolved

She was weak and dreamy, her hand warm in mine as I bent to kiss her goodbye. Mom was ninety-seven years and seven months old. It was mid-July 2014, and she sat in her bed at Bella Vista Transitional Care in San Luis Obispo. I'd come to see her before heading to Paris and Amsterdam with my niece Annie.

"You were always the wild one, Patsy," she said with a smile. "Have a wonderful trip, dear."

I kissed her on the top of the head, said I loved her and would see her when I was back

Mom and I didn't always exist on the same planet, and there are stories about our clashes in this memoir to prove it. As the second of eight children born between 1946 and 1960, arriving on earth in mid-1947, I was the well-timed baby boomer to challenge the world as she knew it. She would rail at me in exasperation and self-righteous conviction, and I would snipe back and argue, defend, and attempt to explain.

Over time, and with many fits and starts, we grew out of it. She conceded later in life with grace and humility that her biggest mistake (or was it her first big mistake?) in parenting me was for-bidding me to see the Beatles at the Hollywood Bowl in 1964 with my girlfriends from Marywood.

She didn't approve of or like most of my friends in grammar school, high school, college, or after. There was always someone she considered odd or a bad influence. She held a special antipathy for my friend Amanda. She opposed my first marriage to a Jewish man officiated by an Episcopalian interfaith chaplain in a Laguna backyard—instead of in the Catholic Church.

"Don't expect any help from me," she'd said.

My future husband Mark and I did all the planning. It went differently for Maureen, Evie, and Paul, who all had church and family-sanctioned weddings (even though Paul refused to get mar-ried at St. Boniface). Mark's parents, who traveled from Bethesda, Maryland, did offer to help. When I told Mom, she jabbed, "So his mother's going to bring a suitcase full of salami for your wedding?"

Really, Mother?

Most of her sisters, except Auntie Evie, boycotted the event. However, lots of "that bunch," her derogatory term for my friends, some of whom drove from the East Coast, were there. To be fair, both my parents and all my siblings did ultimately take part in the celebration.

About a year later, Mom and Daddy decided to leave Anaheim.

If there was any glue that connected the loose particles of our group brain, it was our parents, and particularly Mom. She was the force who made the rules, did the shopping and laundry and cooking, and got us ready for school during the week and Mass on Sundays, making sure all eight of us and Daddy were presentable. We grew up, individuated, got boisterous, got oppositional, had fun, fought, teased, and made shifting alliances. Even though she wanted us to adhere to the familiar family norms, she eventually accepted we had individual needs and idiosyncrasies, and she ac-commodated them as best she could. She insisted we have good manners, were clean and tidy, had directives instilled in us even as on occasion we intentionally fell into disarray. I'm exhausted remembering the job she did.

Paul hated school and was "a nervous little boy." Evie was "high strung" and needed a quiet room. Bobby was "never any trouble." Maureen was an exemplary first child. I was wakeful at night for fear of God coming to me in a vision and asking me to be a martyr. I worried I had a brain tumor. I was terrified of an impending World War III. I went out to Mom late one night crying that I couldn't sleep. She comforted me and took me to a specialist who was confident I didn't have a brain tumor. Why was I so much trouble and bother for her? Johnny, Marguerite, and Michael were not model children, but in my recollection of their younger days, no quirks or flashes of distress from them show on my radar. Were they an inadvertent cohort of the invisible child syndrome? Hmmm.[9]

We are and were creatures of our times (baby boomers), just as Mom was a person of hers (Greatest Generation; post WWI; 1920s; Great Depression). As the fourth of eight children born to Irish parents who traversed the globe and country, living the peripatetic life of many immigrants, Mom found stability in her family. Even though they were middle class and not poor, it took the Sweeney family years and many locales to put down roots: from Derry, Northern Ireland, in 1911, to New Zealand; thence onward to San Francisco and Napa; to Stockton and Ireland again; to Canada and New England; then from Quincy, Massachusetts, to St. Petersburg, Florida; then back to California, finally stopping in Fullerton and Anaheim in 1930. The death of their father, Patrick Joseph, during the Depression in 1935 forced Mom and her older siblings to get jobs and provide for Nana and younger family members. You can read more about this in "The Irish Connection."

---

9   "Dysfunctional Family Roles," Erik Bohlin, M.A., LMHC, accessed February 15, 2025, https://www.erikbohlin.net/handouts/family_roles_dysfunction.pdf.

Mom in the snow with the first four. Early 1950s.

Mom's sense of duty and loyalty to family was profound. When we were growing up on Janss Way, most of her siblings and her own mother, our Nana Sweeney, lived within walking distance (and so did Nana Truxaw and Aunt Carol, Daddy's youngest sister). Mom considered her five sisters to be her best friends, and she was close with her two brothers. It seemed like she was always on the yellow wall phone in the kitchen with one of them or with Nana, whom she called Mama. Over the years my mother, our mother, has been called Mommy, Mother, Mamma, Mom, Patricia, Pat, and Tri (pronounced Tree). I've struggled to consistently call her Mom, probably because my relationship with her changed over time.

~~~~~~

In the summer of 1977, Anaheim was burgeoning with smog and traffic from motels, Disneyland, and new subdivisions and schools. It was no longer a small town. Mom and Daddy started thinking about getting out, getting away.

The Girls in Morro Bay. Top row, from left: Maureen, Evie; bottom row, from left: Mom, me, Marguerite. Around 1980.

At twenty-one, Marguerite was going to college in Oregon. All the older kids were married. Paul lived nearby in Fullerton, the rest of us in the Bay Area. On the surface, we kids were doing well, except for Bobby who, because he was killed in a car crash in 1969, hadn't accompanied brothers and sisters, cousins and peers, as we finished college, started careers, married, and began having children. With seventy-some cousins in the extended families on both sides, there had been and would be an abundance of celebrations, graduations, engagements, and weddings.

Mom quietly ached. The nub of grief that had taken permanent residence in her heart was both sparked and diverted by the many rites of passage. I remember her asking, "Why Bobby? He was such a good boy."

Whether planned or not, Mom was about to reinvent herself. She and Daddy began exploring the Central Coast and liked it. There was a drugstore in Cayucos Daddy thought about buying. Michael was willing to leave Servite, the Catholic boys' school. So, they sold 549 Janss Way and moved with Michael to 175 Formosa Street in the beach tract of Morro Bay, two short blocks from the ocean and 231 miles from the driveway in Anaheim. Michael enrolled at Morro Bay High School for his senior year, the school sitting right above the dunes and beach near Morro Rock. How liberating for Mom to release herself from the proximity of her sisters whose lives at heart were not like hers.

As she settled into new surroundings, in a house and a city clear of family history, she at times wondered if they'd made the right decision. Was it a good move for Bob? Would Michael be better off in a Catholic school? How much would she miss her family? Worry and doubt were in her nature, but it was done; they were there. She was sixty years old, and her sisters and most of her children were now at least four hours away. She could hear the ocean anytime by opening a window or taking a short walk. I imagine her breathing deeply satisfying sighs of relief.

They joined a new parish, St. Timothy's. The pastor, Father Ed (Hoelterhoff), was progressive and provocative, his sermons unsettling and thoughtful, a sharp contrast to the priest at their old parish, St. Boniface. She volunteered at the church, and her mind and heart opened to ideas, cultures, and concerns that were larger than Morro Bay or Anaheim. When I visited, I went to Mass with her and Daddy just to listen to Father Ed's sermons. During Mass he encouraged his parishioners to pray for and care about the world. Mom admired how forthright and kind Father Ed was and had private meetings with him.

She began cooking fish. One of the first times I visited alone, she fixed fresh halibut purchased at a local wharf for dinner. Halibut. We'd grown up eating small hamburger patties and mashed potatoes and canned fruit, a default meal. It was a joke among us kids how many patties Mom could press from one pound of ground round. The patties looked like charcoal briquettes. If we had fish, it was fish sticks on Fridays. Halibut on a Thursday? She was relaxing. She was living in a small beach town, not Disneyland. Michael was making friends. When she asked if I thought they'd done the right thing, the answer was an obvious yes.

They took aqua aerobics at Cuesta, the local community college. She studied and got a real estate license and at sixty-two went back to work, retiring in her eighties. She loved showing houses. Often when we visited, she was away at the office or an open house, or she had paperwork spread out on the dining table. She made it to the Million Dollar Club, an accomplishment at that time. I still have a copy of one of her business cards. We all beamed with pride at her success, at her obvious pleasure in it. Her grief had moved to a quieter place in her heart.

She and Daddy traveled by car and plane to the East Coast and the Pacific Northwest, and to visit us, their kids, scattered around the state. Between us we lived in Fullerton, Carlsbad, Oakland, San Francisco, Bakersfield, Corcoran, Santa Maria, San Jose, Berkeley, Healdsburg, Windsor, Santa Rosa, and maybe more. We were all over the place. Maureen even lived in Kirkland, Washington, for a while. Mom and Daddy visited me one weekend in July 1987 at St. Helena Recovery Center where I was in the rehab program. She loaned me money to go to graduate school. She welcomed Michael's partner, Chance, when they moved down from Portland. She wondered why Johnny had to be gay but got over it. His partner and eventual husband became a cherished member of the family.

When Daddy died in 1995, his funeral was at St. Boniface in Anaheim. A cousin, Father John LeVecke (rather than the pastor we disliked), led the funeral Mass. He said those of us no longer going to church could take Communion and bought the CD of Jackson Browne's "For a Dancer" for Evie and me to play at the burial. The reception was at Nana Truxaw's old house two blocks from Janss Way. Afterward, some of us walked around the old neighborhood. Mom didn't join us, but she was pleased about how Daddy's service turned out.

Mom and I loved shopping together. When I was living in Healdsburg, she asked me to help her find a dress for a nephew's outdoor wedding in steamy hot Bakersfield. We found an elegant orange sherbet sheath at a smart shop in the Healdsburg Plaza. We would go to Dewinkels in Morro Bay for shoes, or Straight Down and Riley's in San Luis Obispo, and lunch at Big Sky Café. We'd get chicken pies at Linn's.

Mom and Marguerite traveled to Italy in a group led by Father Ed. Mom enjoyed the solid house John and I bought near Sebastopol at the end of a country lane above an apple orchard and the Laguna de Santa Rosa. She was pleased when Evie and I married our domestic partners. She enjoyed the company of my mother-in-law Dorothy, who was a Quaker and antiwar tax resister; they were both present when we celebrated at a big party in the backyard, and everyone went to a Giants game in San Francisco the next day. Our moms got special treatment and seats. She was also there for my sixtieth birthday party and took part and cheered when I smashed a piñata of George Bush. If I complained to her about John, my second and final husband, she'd tell me to look for the good.

As I sit with Mom now, writing a piece I tried to avoid by rationalizing that she's embedded in most of the other stories here, I realize how much more I want to tell you about her. I forgot to mention the phone calls and conversations every year around the anniversary of Bobby's birthday and death. We were always in contact on that day, though over time, the conversation shifted to remembrance more than questioning God, to gratitude rather than raw sorrow. That knot of grief morphed into something warm and enriching. Grief is loss and sorrow, but also an opportunity for growth. Given a chance, our mother, Mom, decided to have a life. She evolved.

So many vignettes with her glide through my memory bank. Here are a few where I pushed the pause button.

The time she said, "But dear, you're not an alcoholic anymore!"

"Oh, Mom," I said. "That's not the way it is." I tried to explain that "recovery" is an active word. I don't think she wanted the label applying to me or anyone else in her family (like her father and some of her siblings).

Then, there was an intimacy at Formosa Street just before her ninetieth birthday dinner: I was in the bathroom primping, and she asked if she could come in to put on lipstick. We girls grew up relaxed about sharing bathrooms. I finished with my mascara and watched as she applied color to her lips. She straightened her eyebrows, pinched her cheeks for a little color, and bent to the cupboard beneath the sink to effortlessly grab a can of hairspray. She doused her head several times, swinging the canister with practice and enjoyment. Then she put it away and regarded herself in the mirror, leaning in close, scrutinizing her ninety-year-old face, which was still beautiful to me. "There," she said, still looking closely and smiling. "I'm ready."

Finally, there was the time Evie and I drove Mom and Marguerite to San Diego for Aunt Evie's one hundredth birthday party, about a 350-mile drive each way. Mom was then almost ninety-five and had dementia and other age-related ailments. Patting on moisturizer after her shower, tenderly daubing it on her delicate and thin skin, she commented, "Always sweep the moisturizer up, dear."

"What?" I asked, distracted, focused on getting the job done.

"You want the moisturizer to push your skin up," she explained.

Periodically over the three-day trip, she said something with such clarity that my heart clamped. It was as if her dementia had disappeared, and she was all there.

~~~~~~~

If Mom wasn't the biggest influence in my life, and I'm not saying she wasn't, she was and still is an enormous presence. It was Mom I wanted to please, her approval I sought and fought against. Her anger and disapproval wounded me like no one else's. In my developmental days, as the world was opening to me, I wasn't the nice Catholic girl she'd expected. It cut me to the quick when I felt she didn't see me, didn't see that my intentions were so good, that I wanted the world to be just, that longhaired people weren't bad, that I wasn't having sex or doing drugs (yet). It hurt to wonder whether she truly didn't like or love me. Ironically, after I was in recovery long enough to get a decent car, I eventually became her designated driver, taking her to family gatherings in Anaheim, Newport, or other points south. Marguerite was usually in the back seat napping while Mom and I chatted. It was a gift to spend that time with her.

Even when I was bereft after being laid off from a job I loved, one that I'd hoped to keep for many more years, she never failed to tell me how proud she was of me. She knew what a broken heart felt like. Her deep sympathy bolstered me through the rest of my working life. My own journey was perhaps divinely synchronized with hers so that as life and time went on, we found more inter-sections than differences, and any differences were held in respect and acceptance and even good humor. In the end, she was one of my biggest supporters, and I marveled at her ability to grow. We both grew. She's been gone for ten years, and I still feel her spirit and company. I find myself talking to her.

I don't think any of us missed Anaheim. We were always welcome with partners, dogs, and friends as Formosa Street in Morro Bay became our family home. Marguerite and Michael became full-time residents. The long stretch of beach between Morro Rock and Yerba Buena became part of daily life.

In 2009, Mom stumbled on the broad steps leading down from the kitchen to the family room, fell hard, and broke her hip. She was ninety-two at the time, and that was the beginning of her slow end. All of us gathered around her within twenty-four hours. She endured years of recovery, including bravely showing up for physical therapy while she was able. The anesthesia from the surgery left her bewildered and likely sped up or caused the onset of her dementia. Let this be a warning for all of us.

I thought I'd see her when I returned from the trip to Paris. I was barely back in the country the night she died, but three hundred miles away. The next night, I swear she came into my room to rub my shoulders and tuck me in.

"You were always the wild one, Patsy," she'd said with a smile. Those would be her last words to me.

———

Mom's memorial wasn't in Anaheim but in Morro Bay at St. Timothy's, officiated by Father Ed. He described Mom lovingly, with his typical enthusiasm, saying she was first and foremost a mother. Her grandchildren participated as readers and speakers. Sweeneys young and elderly and a few ex-husbands showed up, and many came by later for dinner. The house on Formosa was full to overflowing that night. It was a splendid gathering, a celebration of life.

Afterword

April 2024

Grief becomes a condition of life, a quality of heart.

A component of treatment at the St. Helena Recovery Center was education about the disease of addiction. We had classes most mornings. I was teachable and receptive by the time I got there. One of the lessons that caught my attention was about the shift in the politics or power relationships in the family when a member gets sober. An active alcoholic or addict puts strain on the best of families, and this often leads to dysfunctionality and triggers the roles of Hero or Savior, Mascot or Clown, Lost or Invisible Child, Scapegoat, and Enabler/Caretaker to surface.[10]

When my bravado, false persona, and sneakiness were replaced by vulnerability, shame, curiosity, loss, and relief after treatment, both friends and family wondered how to see and deal with me. I was no longer a scapegoat or a problem. Fortunately, I had the support of a recovery program and, later, therapy to grow into a healthier self. As one person changes, so does the group. After some initial awkwardness, my getting sober (and doing the work of staying sober) rearranged my place in our family dynamic. It was a slow, cellular-level restructuring. Evie, for example, no longer had to worry about or try to rescue me, which freed up some space in

10   "Dysfunctional Family Roles," Out of the Storm, accessed February 15, 2025, https://www.outofthestorm.website/dysfunctional-family-roles.

her head and improved our relationship. The monkey was off my back. Hurray! Since I'd never properly grieved Bobby's death, I got to do that (and make plenty of amends) after I was forty. It was liberating.

I believe similar shifting and changing occurs when a family member dies, though I only recently made the connection. With Bobby gone, our family group experienced a cellular-level change—more like a rupture. Were we offered therapy, counseling, or some other lens through which to look at what was happening with and to us? No. We had no guide or structure or recovery group to explain the changes. We didn't talk or read about grief and loss. We reacted. Nana Truxaw passed away two months after Bobby. The Vietnam War. Draft concerns for brothers, friends, cousins, the country. We were slammed with sorrows and worry. The result was seven wounded siblings and two parents.

For us "kids" who were still in various stages of development in 1969 (our ages were eight, twelve, sixteen, seventeen, nineteen, twenty-two, and twenty-three), it was bewildering. I feel tenderness for all of us as I look back on the jostling disruption to our spirits and bodies and lives. For Mom and Daddy, it was crushing. Johnny wrote about needing and not receiving comfort.

But it wasn't all bad, was it? I mean, yes, it was horrible to suddenly lose a terrific brother. But we kids would huddle together, get stupid together, drink and party together. As I mentioned in the chapter about Paul, he and I once attempted to meet for happy hour, which is a poignant memory even if we didn't know how to talk to each other.

We were united in enduring Daddy's maudlin speeches during some holiday meals. We joked together about relatives, teased one another, acted out, and grew up. We had weddings, graduations, and careers, and we did a group moonshot that Christmas at Paul's. At least one of the labels above (Hero or Savior, Mascot or Clown, Lost or Invisible Child, Scapegoat, Enabler/Caretaker) might be applicable to some or all of us. If you knew us then or know us now, take your pick. I have my own ideas but won't tell you here. The objective of the book is to honor us for surviving, not to piss anyone off. I'm proud and relieved that we're somehow still talking. We need to talk more.

How we behaved after Bobby died wasn't how we would have had he still been alive. How we behave today isn't how it would be if he were here now.

Over time you almost forget what you're missing. Almost.

This is how, for me, grief became a condition of life and a quality of my heart.

Gathering is a love story to my siblings and parents and a cautionary tale to all readers. The vignettes are connected by behaviors influenced directly or indirectly by the sudden death of a family member. *Gathering* is how I experienced and processed Bobby's death and our individual and collective lives after. No one escaped grief and hurt. Our group reconfigured and frayed, but the core has held. Had we not had a strong connection at the outset, had some of us not had some form of therapy or recovery, however late in life, we might not be so lucky as to still have the impulse to gather.

I'm probably too fond of saying we have bad wiring in our family. That's only part of the story. If I'm being thorough, I must concede that if we're still connected by a common brain, as I believe we are, we have good wiring too.

Family gathered at Newport Beach after Maureen's burial and memorial lunch. December 2017.

Acknowledgements

Gathering was a years-long project incubated, written, and completed with the help and inspiration of many. My deep gratitude to my book shepherds: Sara Roahen, editor and facilitator extraordinaire, and her brilliant partner at Demitasse Press, artist Dorka Hegedus, who did the cover design and interior formatting.

Sonoma County poet and writer Clara Rosemarda's intuitive guidance evoked discovery, experimentation, voice, and confidence, for which I am forever grateful. Her gatherings sparked an offshoot that, thanks to the pandemic, became an ongoing cohort of like-minded women and writers including Judy Baker, Anne Marie Cheney, Heidi Stewart, and me.

I'm indebted to my longtime friend from the '70s, Linda Hanley Finigan, who closely read a draft of the book with love, exclamation marks, and perceptive suggestions.

Life story writing classmates at Cuesta College in San Luis Obispo have been witnesses and cheerleaders for the last five years and motivated me with their own writing.

Copy editor Ceylan Ozguner was precise and caring with the manuscript and a dream to work with. Vanessa Salvia was meticulous with the final proofreading.

My husband John Hansen has been a willing and astute listener and reader of last resort.

Finally, I must acknowledge my sisters, brothers, and parents, whose lives seeded the stories I needed to tell.

About the Author

Patsy Truxaw has been observing and writing about her Irish-Catholic (and partly Czech) family for fifty-plus years. The second of eight children and a baby boomer, Patsy believes she and her siblings inherited some good genes but bad wiring. The bad wiring, compounded by the sudden death of her college-age brother in 1969, is the impetus behind this, her first book. Along with being a lifelong writer, Patsy is a retired educator, a Democrat, and dog lover. She got sober one month after her fortieth birthday and remains active in recovery groups. Patsy lives in Los Osos, California, with her husband John Hansen and their two dogs, Belle and Max.

More at *www.forgivemess.com*.

www.ingramcontent.com/pod-product-compliance
Lightning Source LLC
Chambersburg PA
CBHW051625120626
46551CB00014B/1935